Blackonomic$

The Way To
Psychological and Economic Freedom
For
African Americans

To Jaequeline, Empower our People! Jim

James Clingman
**Author of "Kudos To Black Americans" and
"Economic Empowerment or Economic Enslavement -
We have a choice"**

MILLIGAN BOOKS   CALIFORNIA

Blackonomic$ – The Way To Psychological and
Economic Freedom For African Americans
Copyright © 2000 by James E. Clingman, Jr.
j_cling@fuse.net

First Printing, February 2001
10 9 8 7 6 5 4 3 2 1

ISBN 1-881524-92-2

Published By
Milligan Books, Inc.

Cover Design By
George Hooks

HAIK Publishing
P. O. Box 6722
Cincinnati, Ohio 45206
(513) 489-4132 (Voice or Fax)
www.blackonomics.com
James E. Clingman, Jr.

Milligan Books Inc.,
1425 W. Manchester, Suite B,
Los Angeles, California 90047, (323) 750-3592.
E-mail: drrosie@aol.com   Web site: milliganbooks.com
j_cling@fuse.net

DEDICATION

TO
The memory of Dr. Amos Wilson who, like Booker T. Washington and Marcus Garvey, left us too soon, but whose words I have fed upon and savored to the delight and uplift of my consciousness and my spirit.

TO
Dr. Claud Anderson, a friend and mentor, who suffers inside his soul for his people, is unafraid to speak his message, and unrelenting in his mission to create vehicles for economic empowerment for our people.

TO
Brothers
Ken Price, Curtis Dean, Earvin Johnson,
Ken Bridges, Al Wellington, George Fraser,
Mark Pastor, and John Brown.
You care. You work. You love.

TO
Sisters
Sylvia Clingman
Julianne Malveaux, Brooke Stephens,
Nia Sadika, Maxine Ross,
Dr. Julia Hare, and Rosetta Perry.
You are strength.

The essays herein were written between January 1997 and November 2000. Some have been updated, and others were not. The important consideration for the reader is the fact that the economic empowerment message, whether it's from the 19th century or the 21st century, is <u>Timeless</u>.

Table of Contents

Introduction

Timeless. That's the word that best describes the economic empowerment message, especially as it relates to Black people. Timeless because it has been the watchword for survival in this country since the country began. Timeless because for many years our predecessors have taught us, by example, the basic principles of empowerment, and yet today we still struggle to get it right.

Economic empowerment is like a mathematical equation; it has two sides. If one side is wrong the other side will not work. We must get both sides right in order to move forward. First comes the psychological side of the equation, then the economic side.

The title of this book, **Blackonomics**, ties the two parts of the equation together. Inherent in the name is the fact that economics for Black people is a bit different from that of everyone else in this country. It suggests that we have to do a little more, work a little harder, and move a whole lot faster to achieve our collective economic goals. It is a mindset, in addition to being a system of monetary principles. I suppose I could have called it *"Psychonomics,"* but I wanted everyone to know for whom, about whom, and to whom, this book was written.

Blackonomics may also bring to the minds of those in the know, the term **Powernomics**, which was introduced to us by Dr. Claud Anderson. Understanding the similarity of the terms, I have come up with my own concise definition for both. **Blackonomics** tells us <u>what</u> to do. **Powernomics** tells us <u>how</u> to do it. Both are timeless.

Since our arrival in these United States our quest for freedom has been our highest priority. Now, in the 21st century, we continue our fight for freedom, a fight not against chains and bondage but a fight for freedom of our minds. Many of our people are still psychologically enslaved and, like Harriet Tubman, some of us must have the courage to keep fighting, to keep going back, and to keep up the pressure, until we have built a foundation upon which our children and their children can achieve their true freedom.

It is disheartening to consider the fact that after 400 years, and all we have survived, and all of the lessons passed on to us by our ancestors, we are still fighting for economic freedom. Just whom are we fighting? Who is the enemy? I contend that we are fighting ourselves. I submit to you that we are the enemy, and until we change our minds about one another, it will be very difficult for us to gain economic freedom.

How is it possible for a group of Black people—the most intelligent, the most affluent, and the most spiritual of people - to be as far behind as we are in this country? The answer to that question surely must be grounded in psychological terms because, considering all of the physical resources of African Americans, there can be no other rationale for our lack of economic freedom.

So how do we get our true freedom? We know what the problems are. I will even take it one step further and submit that most of us also know what the solutions are. So, a better question is: Why can't we solve the problem, especially since we already know the answer?

This reminds me of my 9th grade Algebra class. There were problems to which I knew the answers but whose formulas I could not discern. In those cases, even though I had the correct answer, my teacher would mark the problem wrong, because just knowing the answer is not always what's important. We must also know how to attain the answer. Often the activity involved in getting an answer to a problem is what creates the basis from which we learn and, more important, it is what moves us from tentative to habitual.

To sum it all up, we know better. And I say, if we *know better*, and fail to *do better*, then *no better* for us. We are truly suffering from our lack of will and resolve to *do better* when it comes to collective economic empowerment. That is one of the reasons I wrote my **Kudos to Black Americans**, which follows this introduction. I wanted to point out how, despite our tremendous resources and rich legacy, we have failed to execute the economic formula that will get us to the economic answer—even though we know what that answer is. I also wanted to give us a pragmatic reason to reprogram what Brother Ken Bridges calls the "Willie (Lynch) Chip," which was implanted in the minds of African Americans a long time ago.

This book, a *second-time-around* attempt on my part to help us gain our true freedom, reemphasizes the very critical nature of our economic situation. It deals not only with the psychological aspects of economic empowerment but with the practical side as well. It explains in very simple terms what we must do to get our freedom, because it is very simple for us to do so. This book is directional, instructive, proactive in its approach, and even more solution-oriented. It is a collective economic prescription for our collective economic freedom.

The principles of pooling and leveraging resources, directing our tremendous consumption spending toward one another, building and supporting our own businesses, manufacturing, distributing, creating jobs, and land ownership are tried and true economic principles that have propelled many groups to lofty heights of economic empowerment. The failure by Black people to enact those principles, on a collective basis, has plunged us into the depths of despair, self-hatred, distrust, and economic dependence rather than economic independence.

As you read this book, please stop every now and then and think about our past and our future. Think about what you are doing—or not doing—to achieve true freedom for our people. Please do an honest assessment of where you are on the continuum of economic progress for Black people. Are you willing to make the sacrifices necessary for our children's economic future? Are you ready to move from the plantation and help build the economic infrastructure we must have to sustain ourselves as a people? Are you part of the problem or are you part of the solution?

Change your mind if your problem is psychological. Change your actions if you are simply sitting on the side-lines watching the game. Understand that only we can solve our economic problems, and understand that the solution for doing so is very clear. Time is not on our side, so we must act decisively and we must act quickly.

The last essay in this book is titled, **Kudos to Black Americans—A Reprise.** We began the book by describing our problem; we are ending it by providing a solution to that problem. In my daily life I hear many brothers and sisters talk about "what we need to do" and "what they need to do." My question is, "What are you doing?" Merely posing problems and raising issues are not enough. We (each one of us) must be willing to put forth the effort necessary to solve the problems we discuss. Thus, my "Reprise" was written to lift us up, to give us hope, to jumpstart us, and stimulate us to do what we must do to solve our economic problem.

Please commit to loving your brothers and sisters more, trusting them more, and helping them more, and we can look forward to a bright economic future, the basis for every other earthly achievement for which we strive. The message of economic empowerment is indeed timeless, but time is running out. Just as we surely cannot afford to squander our resources, we can hardly afford to squander our time. Internalize! Assess! Transform! Practice! Enjoy!

Prologue

"The Letter"

I wrote the following "Letter" in November 1998 as one of my regular articles for the National Newspaper Publishers Association (NNPA). I saw it as just one in a long line of pieces I had submitted on economic empowerment. I wanted it to slap us in the face with a stark dose of reality and demonstrate, in graphic terms, just how ridiculously flawed our economic practices have been for quite some time now.

After "The Letter To Black Americans" (Titled, **Kudos to Black Americans**) was published by the Philadelphia New Observer newspaper and put on the Internet, it took off and spread like wildfire across the country. "Who could have written this?" was the most frequently asked question. Of course, some people were certain a white person wrote it.

"The Letter" appeared in books and other publications. Minister Fred Price read it on national television at the conclusion of his Race and Religion Series. "The Letter" was the talk of the country. Well, here is the original "Letter" from its original author. I thought it would make an excellent prologue for this book. I hope it stirs you to take appropriate action.

Dear Black Americans:

After all of these years and all we have been through together, we think it's appropriate for us to show our gratitude for all you have done for us. We have chastised you, criticized you, punished you, and in some cases even apologized to you, but we have never formally nor publicly thanked you for your never-ending allegiance and support to our cause.

This is our open letter of thanks to a unique people, a forgiving people, a steadfast people, and a brave people: **Black Americans.**

We will always be in debt to you for your labor. You built this country and were responsible for the great wealth we still enjoy today. Upon your backs, laden with the stripes we sometimes had to apply for disciplinary reasons, you carried our nation. We thank you for that.

We thank you for your diligence and tenacity. Even when we refused to allow you to even walk in our shadows, you followed close behind believing that some day we would come to accept you and treat you like men and women. Your strength in the face of adversity cannot be understated. You are truly a great people, and we thank you so much.

We publicly acknowledge Black people for raising our children, attending to our sick, and preparing our meals while we were occupied with the trappings of the good life. Even during the times when we found pleasure in your women and enjoyment in seeing one of your men lynched, maimed, and burned, some of you continued to watch over us and our belongings. We simply cannot thank you enough.

Your bravery on the battlefield, despite being classified as three-fifths of a man, was and still is outstanding and beyond the call of duty. We often watched in awe as you went about your prescribed chores and assignments, sometimes laboring in the hot sun for twelve hours, to assist us in realizing our dreams of wealth and good fortune. You were always there, and we thank you.

Now that we control at least 90% of all of the resources and wealth of this nation, we have Black people to thank the most. You were there when it all began, and you are still with us today, protecting us from those Black people who have the temerity to speak out against our past transgressions. How can we thank you for your dedication? You warned us about Denmark Vesey; you let us know about Gabriel Prosser's plans; you called our attention to Nat Turner; and you even sounded the alarm when old John Brown came calling on Harper's Ferry. Some of you still warn us even today. Thank you, thank you, thank you!

Now, as we look out upon our enormous wealth, and as we assess our tremendous control of the resources of this country, we can only think of the sacrifices you and your families made to make all of this possible. You are indeed fantastic, and we will forever be in your debt.

To think of how you have looked out for us for hundreds of years and to see you still doing the same thing today is simply amazing. Thank you for continuing to bring 95% of what you earn to our businesses. That is so gracious of you. Thanks for buying our Hilfigers, Karans, Nikes, and all of the other brands you so adore. Your purchase of these products really makes us feel that we are at least giving something back to you for your patronage. After all, in the past the brands we put on you were quite painful, but the brands of today can be proudly worn because they give you a sense of self-esteem, right? But it's the least we can do for a people who have treated us so well.

Your super-rich athletes, entertainers, intellectuals, and business persons (both legal and illegal) exchange most of their money for our cars, our jewelry, our homes, and our clothing. What a windfall they have provided for us! The less fortunate among you spend all they have at our neighborhood stores enabling us to open even more stores. Sure, they complain about us, but they never do anything to hurt us economically. You are a very special people. Thank you.

Oh yes, allow us to thank you for not bogging yourselves down with the business of doing business with your own people. We can take care of that for you; please don't trouble yourselves with it. Yes, you were very successful at it after slavery ended and even as recently as 1960, but you know what happened when you began to build your own communities and do business with one another. Some of the "lower ones" of our kind burned you out—time and time again. So why bother? In today's business environment your own people will not support you anyway.

You just keep doing business with us; it's safer that way. Besides, everything you need, we make anyway, even Kente Cloth. You just continue to dance and sing and fight and get high and go to prison and backbite and envy and distrust and hate one another. Have yourselves a good time, and this time we'll take care of you. It's the least we can do, considering all you've done for us. Heck, you deserve it, Black people.

For your labor which created our wealth, for your resisting the messages of trouble-making Blacks like Washington, Delaney, Garvey, Bethune, Tubman, and Truth, for fighting and dying on our battlefields, we thank you. For caring for our families, for abandoning your own businesses and business organizations, we deeply thank you. For allowing us to move into your neighborhoods and for your patronage of our businesses, we will forever be grateful to you. For your unceasing desire to be near us and for hardly ever following through on your threats due to our lack of reciprocity and equity—we thank you so much.

We also appreciate your acquiescence to our political agendas, for abdicating your own economic self-sufficiency, and for working so diligently for the economic wellbeing of our people. You are real troopers. And even though the 13th, 14th, and 15th Amendments were written for you, many of your relatives having died for the rights described therein, you did not resist when we changed those *Black rights* to *civil rights* and allowed virtually every other group to take advantage of them as well. Black people, you are something else!

Your dependence upon us to do the right thing is beyond our imagination, irrespective of what we do to you and the many promises we have made and broken. But this time we will make it right, we promise. Trust us.

Tell you what. You don't need your own hotels. You can continue to stay in ours. You have no need for supermarkets when you can shop at ours 24 hours a day. Why should you even think about owning more banks? You have plenty now. And don't waste your energies trying to break-in to manufacturing. You've worked hard enough in our fields. Relax, have a party; we'll sell you everything you need. And when you die, we'll even bury you at a discount. Now how's that for gratitude?

Finally the best part—and we are so appreciative. You went beyond the pale and turned your children over to us for their education. With what we have taught them, it's likely they will continue in a mode similar to the one you have followed for the past 45 years. When Mr. Lynch walked the banks of the James River in 1712 and said he would make us a slave for 300 years, little did we realize the truth in his prediction. Just thirteen more years and his promise will come to fruition. But with two generations of your children having gone through our education systems, we can look forward to at least another fifty years of prosperity. Wow! Things could not be better—and it's all because of you.

For that, and for all you have done, we thank you from the bottom of our hearts, Black Americans. You're the best friends any group of people could ever have!

Sincerely,

All Other Americans

Section One

Our Proud History

The conditions of today have been determined by what has taken place in the past, and in a careful study of this history we may see more clearly the great theatre of events in which the Negro has played a part. We may understand better what his role has been and how well he has functioned in it.
Carter G. Woodson

Everything stems from something in the past. Each one of us has come from someone else. Our history is very important and, in considering the proper order of all things, we must begin there.

It is vital that we learn and heed the lessons taught us by our elders – those who have passed on and those who are yet with us. But too often our people get stuck in the past and never really deal with the present. Some of us revel in the fact that we were kings and queens, that we ruled vast empires, and that we built the pyramids. While all of that is true, we simply continue to dream and reflect upon the past. We must turn our attention as well to the present and future of our people.

We cannot stop with celebrations of the building of the pyramids. We must use those celebrations as springboards and build some pyramids of our own. The pyramids of Y2K for Black people must be institutions, hotels, banks, warehouses, supermarkets, and the like.

Our history is replete with examples of how to take care of business. Our predecessors built their own cities, their own companies, their own communities, and their own lives to reflect the kind of determination, resolve, and tenacity we should model today.

Ours is a beautiful tapestry of the experiences of men and women, free and enslaved, who knew that "doing for self" was the only way to survive in this foreign land. They knew that by using their God-given talents, working together, supporting one another, and making sacrifices, they would eventually possess their own land and live by "our own efforts," as William Wells Brown declared.

Why do these words of true wisdom seem to have fallen on deaf ears? Martin Delaney, Marcus Garvey, and Booker T.

Washington surely cannot be resting in peace. After all, they and others laid the groundwork for us to follow and we are still trying to get it right. We must change.

Additionally, as we remember Garvey et al for their contributions to the economic empowerment of Black people, there are two elder sisters I have included in this section. Ida B. Wells and Rosa Parks, not known for their economic empowerment work, but for their defiance, their strength, and their commitment to their people, are included as well. I thought it appropriate to add articles I had written about these giants to this section because of their positive historical impact and the lessons they taught us—and because I love them.

The lessons of our ancestors are ours to heed. Our history demands that we move beyond rhetoric and begin following them. Hear the words of our forefathers and mothers in these next few chapters. Heed their words. Make them proud. Make your children proud.

A Re-call to Action

In my speeches and writings I always try to impress upon my audience that the things I say and write are not new. Rather, my words are merely old messages wrapped in new packaging—old medicine in new bottles. Everything I do regarding economic empowerment is a reiteration of what great men and women have told us for 200 years. In other words, my message is simply a re-call to action for our people, a re-emphasis on the most important aspect of our survival in this country: Economic empowerment.

We hear a great deal of rhetoric about freedom. It has been the topic of conversation since we were brought to this country. Other people talked about freedom as well, and they used our ancestors to gain that freedom by having them work their entire lives without paying for their labor. The freedom sought by those who brought our people to these shores was grounded in economics. True freedom - in America today - is still economic freedom, but it begins with psychological freedom.

True freedom was the call of our ancestors, and they still cry out from their graves for us to be the men and women for whom they lived and died. They wanted us to use their sacrifices to make our road a little less rocky, and they wanted us to pass that same drive and direction on to our children. They left institutions here for us and they wanted us to leave a similar legacy for our children. What do you think they would say if they could return and see us in our current economic condition in these United States, in whose soil their blood is soaked?

A re-call to action? That's exactly what we need—and we need to act upon this call, once and for all, to gain the benefits to which we are not only entitled but must have if we are going to remain in this country. Our true freedom is at stake. Every other group is getting theirs or has already gained it—with our patronage, our labor, and our blood. Now that we have empowered everyone else, don't you think it's time to empower ourselves?

21

In 1847,when Frederick Douglass moved to Rochester, New York and started his own newspaper, *The North Star*, he was determined to publicize his views on slavery. He continued his arduous calling of speaking out and informing his people—as well as others—about the current state of affairs in this country. After slavery ended, Douglass was just as outspoken regarding what the country needed to do to bring about "equality" for its new citizens.

On the other hand, the lady they called "Black Moses," Harriet Tubman, was not of the same opinion as Douglass. She believed the newly freed slaves needed much more than the vote in order to have true freedom. She made numerous trips back to slave territory to bring her brothers and sisters to freedom and was so passionate about her mission and her message that she did it sometimes with a firearm pointed at those she was rescuing.

Black abolitionist, Sojourner Truth, spoke out and carried the message of freedom wherever she traveled. Ida B. Wells, 70 years before our beloved Rosa Parks made her famous statement, refused to sit in a segregated train car. She won her suit against the Chesapeake and Ohio Railroad and was awarded $500 in damages.

Moving into the 20th century, beginning with Booker T. Washington's National Negro Business League, the message of economic freedom began to take hold among Black people. Others followed Washington's lead. Marcus Garvey, Martin Delaney, Madam C.J. Walker, Mary McLeod Bethune, Elijah Muhammad, Martin Luther King, and Malcolm X all promoted this thing called economic empowerment. Black towns were established in the 1800's and Black communities were thriving as late as the 1960's. Our ancestors knew where they had to go. Even though they were taking different roads to get there, they knew their ultimate cause was true freedom—economic freedom.

What happened to that message since 1964? For 36 years we have seemingly ignored the basic principles of collective and cooperative economics and gone our separate ways as a people in this country. Black people have embraced the illusion of "political power" in exchange for an even more important possession: economic power. For nearly four decades we have languished in political purgatory thinking we would be all right if we could just get some Black people elected to public office. Well, we have elected some 9000 Black people to office, and what do we have to show for it economically?

This re-call to action is about what our real leaders have told us to do all along. They told us to get some land, be producers, establish businesses, recycle our dollars, and support our businesses. They told us to determine our own destiny, to take care of ourselves and not be dependent upon others, to be men and women who will stand up for our rights and not be swayed by a few dollars, a "good job," or a high-status position. They told us to love, trust, and care for one another and to leave something here that will make our children proud.

A re-call to action must begin with a look back. It must begin with our acceptance of the fact that we are a great people having evolved from an even greater people. Our re-call to action must be immersed in the principles and examples set forth by our people; it must be attached to the goal of gaining our true freedom, both psychological and economic.

We must accept the fact that there are no new complicated strategies for us to develop and have endless meetings about; there are no new business principles we must learn; and there are no new economic formulas that will keep us up late at night trying to decipher. There are three simple things we must obtain and use wisely and collectively in order to achieve our goal: Land, labor, and capital. The last time I checked, we had plenty of labor (40 million Black people in the U.S.) and capital ($500 billion per year). Admittedly, we are a little short on land, but America is for sale. Just ask the Japanese people.

This re-call to action is an alarm for those Black people who could, if they were so inclined, change the economic landscape simply by practicing some of the precepts passed on to us by Booker T. Washington and Marcus Garvey. The super-rich among us could lead the masses out of economic despair if they were simply willing to speak out publicly on our behalf and pool just a portion of their dollars to help build our communities. Our army of consumers could lower the profit margins of major corporations simply by refusing to buy their products—not for one day but for one year or more, if they were so inclined.

Our politicians, if they were so inclined, could be less concerned with their individual popularity and their re-election, and more involved in substantive issues—economic issues—and change the perception held by some of our young people who might enter the political arena. Our "leaders" of organizations and movements could concentrate on economic empowering strategies—collective rather than individual—and move our people beyond our current economic position, if they were so inclined. Considering the fact that many of those "leaders" have squandered the last 35 years, in terms of economic empowerment, they have a lot of catching up to do.

Yes, this is a re-call to action for Black people, and this time we had better heed the call. One hundred and thirty-five years removed from slavery, one hundred years after the founding of the National Negro Business League, thirty-two years after the assassination of Martin Luther King. How much longer do we expect to slumber? How many more Black lives must be destroyed before we decide to change our ways? How much more of our money are we willing to give away before we obtain the reciprocity we deserve? How long are we going to wait before we begin to build an economic legacy for our children?

In my first book, **Economic Empowerment or Economic Enslavement – *We have a choice,*** I stress the tremendous resources we have among our people, the proud history and people from which we have come, and the very important fact that we do have a choice. Our ancestors, when they were brought to this country, had to choose between living and dying. Our choices today are

24

miniscule in comparison to theirs. We simply must choose between empowerment and enslavement when it comes to how we use our economic and intellectual resources.

If we make the right choices we will make our ancestors proud. For the past thirty-five years we have made the wrong choices. We chose political gain over economic gain and began the longest boycott in the history of this country—Black consumers against Black owned businesses. We chose to walk away from our businesses and patronize businesses owned by everyone else. We chose to abdicate our responsibility to our children and turn them over to someone else for their education. We chose to seek individual rather than collective economic gain. In other words, we chose economic slavery rather than economic empowerment.

Be encouraged in knowing, however, that we do have another chance. Although our window of opportunity is swiftly closing, we can still get it right. We need the commitment of likeminded individuals who have reached a level of consciousness that will steer us to true freedom. This group of foot soldiers will work despite the absence of the spotlight and the cameras, despite the lack of public acknowledgement, and despite their lack of notoriety and accolades.

These dedicated individuals will adopt the persona of Harriet Tubman, as described in Frederick Douglass' tribute to the Black Moses. *I have had the applause of the crowd and the satisfaction of being approved by the multitude, while the most that you have done has been witnessed by the few trembling, scarred, foot-sore bondmen and women whom you have led out of the house of bondage... The Midnight sky and silent stars have been the witnesses of your devotion to freedom and of your heroism.*

True freedom will come to our people if we are willing to be Harriet Tubmans—and Marcus Garveys, and Booker T. Washingtons, Martin Luther Kings, and Malcolm X's. We must be willing to work, not for the fanfare, but because it is the right thing to do—for ourselves and our children.

We have heard many re-calls to action from the giants of our time. This is yet another recall, not from a giant or a celebrity or a politician or one of our important national "leaders." This re-call comes from a Black man who simply loves his people and yearns for the day when most of us are marching in lock-step toward true economic and psychological freedom. Won't you answer the call this time?

Words Without Action Are Just Words.

I often think about how we recite the words of famous Black people after they have passed away. It's sad to think that so many of our predecessors said so many important and enlightening things that we failed to heed or even repeat until long after their death.

I hope my words are not merely quoted and used to simply stir the emotions—now or after I have left this earth. Too often we let opportunity slip away because we fail to act upon information when we receive it; we'd rather wait and use the words to temporarily satisfy and soothe our pains.

Let's look at some examples. In the past decade or two, the phrase *By any means necessary* has been used millions of times by our brothers and sisters. Had we followed some of Malcolm's words at the time he was saying them, imagine where we would be today. Still many Black men and women quote him and use his words to stir the emotions, but few are willing to incorporate the words into their daily lives. How many of us are willing to have economic strength *by any means necessary?*

Marcus Garvey is another brother who is quoted quite often. Remember, *Up you mighty race...?* How many of us actually live by his words? What about Mary McCleod Bethune? She told us what to do economically before she died, and we just love to hear her words today. Have we turned her words into action? Martin Delaney, T. Thomas Fortune, William Wells-Brown, Harriet Tubman, Ida B. Wells, and many more have told us what we must do for ourselves in order to have a strong economic foundation. Are we following the principles they espoused?

Let us not forget about Booker T. Washington, who practiced what he preached and demonstrated, before our very eyes, the results of his words. And probably the most quoted of them all, Frederick Douglass, who told us what to do and how to do it more than 100 years ago. We love to talk about "Power" and how it *concedes nothing*, and we rejoice in his notion of *agitation.*

Are we merely interested in feeling good about economic empowerment? Do we just like to hear the words of these—and more—famous Black men and women? Or, are we willing to act upon those words as well? Speakers can recite the words of famous people and bring the audience to a high level of excitement, but if the audience goes home and does not act upon those words, they become, as another famous writer and activist named Paul said, *Sounding brass and tinkling cymbals.*

As we face our collective economic future, we can look at it in one of two ways: As a speeding train about to run over us or as a train we are about to board and take for a nice long trip. What's it going to be? If we had followed a few of the words our mothers and fathers uttered when they walked this earth, I shudder to think how powerful we would be, how together we would be, how truly rich we would be, not only financially but in most other ways as well. Additionally, since we are talking about that train, we certainly would not have to worry about it running us down— we'd own it!

The thousands of you who read this article and those who have read other columns I have written, please don't sit back after reading them and simply say, "Man, that was right on the money," or something to that effect. If these words make you "feel good" please allow them to make you "do good" as well.

My words are not new words; I have borrowed them from many great Black brothers and sisters. They have been recycled more times than we'd like to count. So when are we going to heed them? When are we going to act? Some say information is power—but I say information is only power if it is acted upon. If you have been reading my column, you have the information. If this is the first time you have seen it, you will get more information in future articles. Either way, it is up to you to act. It is up to you to find your niche and do what you can for our people. It is up to you to be an active participant in collective economic empowerment.

In the 1950's, Horace Sudduth said, *Economic freedom is the greatest cause before the Negro today.* In the 1960's, Martin Luther King said, *The emergency we now face is economic.* In 1912, Booker T. Washington said, *Let us act, before it's too late—before others come from foreign lands and rob us of our birthright.* The key word is **ACT**. Please do not allow the words of our glorious ancestors to go unheeded.

Black Economic History – Tell That Story Too.

During February, we are deluged with the images and sounds of our people as they struggled to win their freedom. We will revisit, via our television sets and newspapers, the stories of how we have come so far and are still striving to "overcome." We will hear tales of a people who, despite the tremendous odds they faced, fought and died for their right to vote, their right to eat in the restaurants of others, and their right to sit where they pleased on any bus.

We will hear many speeches, take more pop quizzes on Black inventors, memorialize the Underground Railroad, and watch Shaka Zulu a few times. In 1998 a report on National Public Radio did a feature on a play being planned in Bridgeport, Connecticut in commemoration of Black History Month. The musical was titled, "Hang Him From a Tree," (maybe it was a take-off of Lady Day's Strange Fruit) and it covered the gamut of Black history, at least the parts that make some of us angry and others "uncomfortable," as one of the white performers said in an interview.

Oddly, this play was billed as an event that would bring the races together, especially because of its mixed cast (Blacks and whites). Why can't we bring the races together with business deals and economic development? It's always about "talking" rather than real action.

We have had "dialogues on race" and we continue to have conversations on race all over the country as we desperately attempt to mend the torn (or should I say ripped?) racial fabric of the United States. With all that we have done and all we will do this month, we should be well on our way to fixing this "race" problem we face and I hope we do. But Black history is not all about "race." It's also about Black business.

So enough of the condescending commercials, the same tired euphemisms, the weak attempts to regurgitate one aspect of Black history, and the concentration throughout the month on merely *feel-good* vignettes and **what we should do** scenarios. How about some Black history like the spot I heard last year? Actor Dorian Harewood did a spot on a little known Black man who advocated self-help and business development. His name is Martin Delaney, Businessman. Now that's Black history!

I want our children to hear about Black men and women who showed us the way to economic self-sufficiency. I want them to know more about our people than I knew when I was growing up and attending school. They should not only learn about slavery and civil rights, they should be very familiar with Mary McLeod Bethune, S.B. Fuller, Madam C.J. Walker, Anthony Overton, Phillip Payton, Isaiah T. Montgomery, and A.G. Gaston. I also want them to know about Cincinnati's famous Black entrepreneur, Horace Sudduth, who served as the President of National Negro Business League in the 1940's and 1950's and owned the nationally famous Manse Hotel.

We must not continue to allow our history to be told with omissions of the economic strides Black people have made. Our history is an array of achievements, rich in progress and milestones. It is a full-feature documentary of economic enterprise. Our history is a tapestry of self-determination, sacrifice, and resolve, especially when it comes to business.

We must tell the complete story and not be lulled to sleep by tales of woe and racism and the "can't we all get along" mantra of Rodney King. Be not deceived by the outward trappings of our African heritage co-opted by persons who have no genuine interest in our progress. And be wary of the commercialization of Black History Month by those merely interested in ripping off another Black dollar.

Tell your children about our forefathers and mothers who built towns, opened banks and insurance companies, established colleges, sold and developed real estate, started beauty and barber shops, funeral parlors, and built hotels, like Horace Sudduth did in Cincinnati.

Talk to your children about the great Black men and women who took the risks and built wealth in their communities. They were brave souls too, you know. If you have not heard of these and the many other Black economic pioneers, make Black History Month a month of reading and learning about these men and women. Then teach your children. They need business role models too. They need to know they can *just do it.*

Let's define our own history, not only in terms of struggle but also in terms of triumph. Let us always acknowledge the contributions made by Fred Shuttlesworth and understand as well the economic victories of Horace Sudduth. Let's tell the whole story. Then let's take that glorious history of ours and make our ancestors proud, not merely by remembering and celebrating their accomplishments but also by emulating their spirit of economic self-help. If they could do all they did in their day, just imagine the possibilities we have in our day.

Black business is Black History too.

Tuskeegee University – Black Americans' Economic Mecca

I had the pleasure of being the keynote speaker for the third annual Booker T. Washington Economic Summit held at Tuskeegee University's Kellogg Center. The Center, another story of empowerment in and of itself, is one of the best conference centers in the country—right in the middle of a Black college campus.

First of all, I must thank Drs. Ntam Baharany and Velma Blackwell for asking me to speak at this prestigious event. Although I had planned to attend as a conferee, my visit to the historic campus was even more significant to me because of their confidence in me as a speaker for the Awards Banquet.

As I thought about the history of Tuskeegee University, juxtaposed against the current status of the school, it struck me that we—Black people—should revere this institution as the birthplace of economic empower-ment. We should cherish this school where giants walked and instructed our people to "do for self." Each of us should make an annual pilgrimage to the campus if for nothing more than to view the pictorial display of Dr. George Washington Carver's amazing achievements or to simply sit and reflect on what actually has taken place on those grounds since 1881.

I thought about the fact that we as Black people have never seemed to "get it" when it comes to the messages of economic empowerment, especially those from Booker T. Washington. I thought about all of the learned brothers and sisters who graduated from Tuskeegee and who are now in every corner of the world and involved in virtually every kind of business. And then I wondered how many of those persons make regular donations to the school—their school—to keep its beacon shining throughout the world.

I also thought about the Kellogg Center, a well-managed, top-of-the-line hotel and conference center in which we see Black employees working and serving the finest food—even a spicy soup made of sweet potatoes to commemorate their many uses discovered by Dr. Carver. I wondered if Black organizations were aware of the Center and if they were utilizing the Center for their meetings. After all, the room rates cannot be beat, and the feeling of just being "at home" is something with which other establishments cannot compete.

Moreover, as Tony Brown and others have suggested, why shouldn't our Black organizations plan meetings at Black colleges and put the millions spent each year on conferences into those institutions? This is especially meaningful if we are unwilling to forego our annual conferences for one year and pool our funds to build Black owned hotels. Please, somebody stop me before I start making sense.

Back to the Economic Summit. This is a national call for everyone interested in economic empowerment—and all Black people should be—to get in touch with the folks at Tuskeegee University and obtain more information on the Summit. In addition, we must explore ways in which we can support this valuable institution and maintain the principle on which it was founded—self-help through Black business development. We cannot continue to turn our heads the other way when it comes to doing something for ourselves collectively. We are too far behind now, and we have a lot of catching up to do. We have the resources, both financial and intellectual, so what are we waiting for?

The Awards Banquet was inspiring and motivating as five outstanding Black business persons received recognition for their accomplishments.

I listened attentively to Mr. Charles McAfee, of Wichita, Kansas. An architect for 30 years, as he discussed his willingness to fight even more for Black economic empowerment. I was filled with admiration for this successful Black man as he stood and said he will continue to assist other Black businesses and individuals in our quest for economic unity.

As I listened to Mr. James Paschal speak, my thoughts went back to 1976 when I took a group of high school students to visit Clark University, stayed at Paschal's Hotel, and enjoyed the hospitality of a fine Black—owned restaurant. Paschal and his brother are models of self-help, and the Atlanta community that supported and helped maintain their business for so many years is exemplary of true economic empowerment.

And then there was "Connie" Harper, a second-generation Tuskeegee graduate whose mother was instructed by George Washington Carver. She is the fire-brand from Montgomery, Alabama who started the first rural Opportunities Industrialization Center (OIC) in 1968. She is still going strong as a housing and training advocate for the less fortunate in her city.

There was a young man named Alfonso Robinson who operates a family owned pharmacy in Tuskeegee. He deservedly received an award for his tenacity and for doing something we rarely find in our communities—carrying-on in the family business.

And finally there was "Shorty" Miller. This man provided food and a social setting for the students of Tuskeegee for many years. Those who attended the school will remember "The Block" and certainly Mr. Emanuel Marx Miller who thought so much of others that he often used his personal resources for their benefit. He is indeed a role model for our people.

The Booker T. Washington Economic Summit will reconvene next year. I hope to see many more attendees, and I will do whatever I can to assist the planners in their efforts to conduct another successful event. It is vitally important that we get serious about economic empowerment. It is the only mechanism through which Black people will realize our tremendous untapped economic potential. We must move beyond the divisions among us and move toward unity. As Booker T. said, *We must not allow our grievances to overshadow our opportunities.*

Black brothers and sisters, we must adopt a national economic strategy that will benefit our people and understand that we cannot be everything to all people. Black people must help Black people, just as other groups help their own people. And this has nothing to do with disliking anyone else; rather it has to do with loving your own people and being concerned about the future of our children. If you honestly think about it, you must admit that despite our strategy of the past forty or so years, Black people have remained locked-in to a no-win situation when it comes to economics. We must change this scenario, and we can change it by adopting the plan being promoted by Dr. Claud Anderson, author of **Black Labor, White Wealth** and **Powernomics**. We can change by listening to others like T.M. Pryor, author of **Wealthbuilding Lessons of Booker T. Washington – for a New Black America.**

Folks, the instructions have been given to us for 100 years. Unfortunately, much of Washington's work in economic empowerment has been overlooked and hidden from our view, but we need not remain in the dark. We have several great books available to us, and we do not have to reinvent the wheel when it comes to empowering ourselves. All we need to do is adopt a national strategy, and on the way to that national plan of action, adopt local strategies via the oldest Black business organization in this country—the National Business League or Black Chambers of Commerce.

We have much work to do. We can start by supporting Tuskeegee University's Economic Summit. Plan to make your pilgrimage to that hallowed ground—our Mecca, and get involved, on some level, in economic empowerment for Black people. Our future depends upon it.

Why Not Another Black Wall Street?

I am sure you have read or heard the news about the call for Black people to invest more. Brother Jackson is on the case from Wall Street in New York to Silicon Valley in California, buying shares and suggesting we do the same. Carol and Duane Davis have decided to take their Coalition of Black Investors Seminars on the road. And there are many more brothers and sisters promoting increased investments by Black people. Good idea?

Yes, to a certain degree. If we are going to create individual wealth we must invest and be prepared to stay in for the long haul. It's certainly not about Passbook Savings Accounts or even Certificates of Deposit anymore. They are *passé* and, quite frankly, rip-off accounts, considering how much we end up paying banks for "extra charges" and interest on their loans. In that scenario we can do nothing but lose. So, yes, investing is a good idea.

Investment clubs are an excellent way to get started in the stock market, and being no expert I will stop there. Go see a financial manager or a stockbroker—a Black one, of course, and let him or her guide you through that process. But, yes, do plan to invest some of your money and get in on the Wall Street gravy train. Traditionally Black people have stayed away from stocks as if they were esoteric commodities reserved only for the rich. Well, how do you think many of those persons got rich in the first place? Bingo!

As I said, I agree with this latest strategy to invest, to buy shares of stocks, to have a "voice" in corporate America. My admonition is that we do not put all of our eggs in one basket. By investing all of our dollars in Wall Street, we end up doing what we have been doing far too long, that is, creating wealth for someone else. Have you ever wondered why those white men and women, standing on that balcony at the New York Stock Exchange always clap and cheer when the market closes? You got it. Sure, individual Black people will be better off as a result of their "diversified portfolios," but will Black people in general be better off?

I say, while we are investing in Fortune 500's, trying to make a killing in the market, we should and must also be willing to invest in our own neighborhoods, in our own businesses, in ourselves. Why can't we recreate our own Black Wall Street? We like to brag on the one in Tulsa, Oklahoma back in the 1920's, but too many of us are willing to simply let it remain little more than a pleasant memory.

My contention is that while we are putting all of our eggs in the Blue Chip basket and in the baskets of businesses owned by everyone other than Black people, especially Black people in our own communities, we are simply perpetuating our own collective economic decline.

Without ownership we are nothing in this country, and consider this: T.M. Pryor says, *If the Black business establishment disappeared from the American scene this moment, the American stock market would not react one smidgen.* What does that say for Black business clout? What does it say for our economic position in this country? Besides, how much of a "voice" can we have in Microsoft, Intel, IBM, Procter and Gamble, and General Motors anyway? We could invest several million dollars and our "voice" would still be a mere "whisper" among the din in those corporate boardrooms.

If we do not also invest in ourselves and create Black Wall Streets all over this country, we will create individual Black affluence, but our collective economic clout will remain status quo. In every Black neighborhood there are potential and real projects that can be funded by Black people for Black people, you know, the way the Jewish people do it, the way the Asian people do it.

How about pooling some Black funds via a Limited Liability Corporation and creating wealth through economic development in "The Hood," the way the brothers are doing on the West Side of Atlanta to the tune of $130 million? Or, how about making it a weekly habit to pool your funds in your local Black financial organization (if you have one) and invest them from time to time in small business development?

Here's one last investment strategy for us. Invest your dollars in Black attorneys, doctors, grocers, photographers, computer technicians, consultants, financial planners, sports agents, media outlets, and all the rest. That's what our people did in Oklahoma, Philadelphia, and Durham way back when. That's how they built their own Black Wall Street. Why can't we do it again? I think we can. If we do not allow ourselves to be lured totally away from our collective agenda, we can have Black Wall Streets once again.

"Booker T. Washington's Vision for our People"
A speech by James Clingman, October 15, 1998

Good evening, Ladies and Gentlemen. It is a true honor to have been asked by Dr. Baharany to speak to you during this economic summit. While my first intention was to come and learn more about the teachings of Booker T. Washington and to network with new friends, this is certainly a unique opportunity, and I am humbled by it.

As I thought about what I would say to you tonight, the theme of this conference struck me. The subtitle, *"Revisiting Booker T. Washington's blueprint for economic empowerment,"* suggests that we have been here before; we have visited his ideas prior to this conference. Well, I am suggesting that we stop *visiting.* Let's kick off our shoes and stay a while this time. We must adopt the teachings of Booker T., practice them and stop merely giving them lip service every now and then.

As I walked around this campus the last time I was here I felt I was on hallowed ground. We are standing on the shoulders of giants who walked this same ground and did their part in passing on a legacy of self-reliance and self-determination among Black people. We must do our part. Tuskeegee University should be the Mecca of economic empowerment for our people; we should make annual pilgrimages to this place to learn, to reflect, and to put into practice what many of us only celebrate once a year— Ujamaa—cooperative economics, and Ujima—collective work and responsibility.

By the way, my great-grandmother married a man named Toliaferro from the same area of Virginia as Booker lived. So I have surmised that Booker T. and I are distant cousins because of that same slave owner named Toliaferro, Booker's middle name.

I'd like to read you one of my favorite quotes from Booker T. *Now is the time, not in some far-off future, but now is the time, for us as a race to prove to the world that... we have the ability and the inclination to do our part in*

40

owning, developing, manufacturing, and trading in the natural resources of our country. If we let these golden opportunities slip from us in this generation, I fear they will never come to us in like degree again. Let us act... before it's too late, before others come from foreign lands and rob us of our birthright.

For me, this statement captures the essence of Booker T's concern and urgency for Black people to become economically empowered. His prediction, of course, has come true but it still speaks so clearly to what we must do even today—some 76 years after he spoke those words. Booker T. was certainly preaching to the choir, and I do the same thing. But as I always say, I don't mind preaching to the choir, because everybody in the choir is not converted. When we start preaching to the *converted*, we will have lived up to the legacy of Booker T. Washington.

What was Booker T. talking about? What did he really want us to do? Well, one of the most important things he wanted for his people is **Solidarity.** He also wanted us to cooperate with one another. Those are two vitally important aspects for any people to embrace—much less Black people. If we are going to make the kind of progress we must make to survive in this country, we must stick together and share our resources—not just financial resources but intellectual resources as well.

Booker T. also wanted us to concentrate on wealth-building. He wanted us to realize the importance of owner-ship and work toward having businesses rather than mere jobs. I always say, We all had jobs when we got off the boats that brought us here. It was full employment for Black people. Then President Lincoln "fired" the slaves in what was the largest downsizing in history. Jobs are merely on loan to us; they can be taken back virtually anytime; they cannot be passed on to our children—but businesses can be passed. At a time when the net worth of Black people is ten times less than that of white people, we should pay even closer attention to what Booker T. was saying about wealth-building.

Washington also wanted us to build and maintain our own institutions, especially educational (schools) and business (chambers of commerce or business leagues). He suggested that local chapters of the National Negro Business League be our local Chambers of Commerce.

Booker T. wanted us to own land. He said, "A landless people are like ship without a rudder." He was quite impressed to see that in the first decade of the twentieth century Black people went from $177 million to $493 million in land ownership. I am sad to report that Black people once owned 20 million acres of land in this country. Now that total is down to a mere 400,000 acres, according to the latest report by the Harvest Institute in Washington, DC. Booker warned us that we would go the way of Haiti and Liberia if we did not take advantage of the land we possessed by developing the soil, mines, and forests. Those two countries did not take care of their land, rather the people relied upon someone else to provide for them—and the rest is history, as they say.

Be producers, Booker said. *Get land and lie on it. You go to town with your wagon empty and return with the wagon full and your pockets empty. You must go to town with your wagon full of your produce and come back with your wagon empty and your pockets full.*

He wanted Black people to hold mortgages. *Let us knit business and industrial relations into those of the white man,* Booker said, *Till a Black man gets a mortgage on a white man's house that he can foreclose at will. The white man on whose house the mortgage rests will not try to prevent that Negro from voting when he goes to the polls.*

Brother Washington wanted us to learn trades—to be generalists instead of specialists. He introduced Brick-making to Tuskeegee in 1883, Carpentry in 1884, Printing in 1885, Mattress and Cabinet-making in 1887, Wagon-building in 1888, and Shoemaking and Tinsmithing in 1889. Booker T. wanted us to *participate* in the market and not *be* the free market. I often say that the free market is the Black market, because we give it away. Black people have an annual income of $469 billion, 95% of which is spent with businesses other than our own. Someone is living on two incomes, 100% of theirs and 95% of ours, and we ask why we are behind.

Booker T. Washington was also a very spiritual man. He believed in and practiced the highest of morals. But he did not believe *in pie in the sky, by and by, when I die* kind of religion. He told his followers not to ignore the present because they had faith in the future. *With the exception of preaching the gospel of Christ,"* he stated, *"there is no work that will contribute more largely to the elevation of the race in the south than a first-class business enterprise.*

Finally, Booker T. believed we should build our economic base first before we chased political appointments. He taught that by building strong families and developing economic power we would lay the groundwork for our political involvement, and we would not have to go looking for it. The politicians would find us. He was right again. *During the first 50-100 years of the life of any people, are not the economic occupations always given the greater attention?* he asked.

Despite what you have heard about the debate between W.E.B. DuBois and Booker T. regarding economics and politics, we missed the boat on what both men were saying. We should have taken the best of both of these giants instead of playing into the hands of those who would keep our people divided. We did not have to choose between the two men. We could not afford divisions among our people then, nor can we afford them now, but subversion is always with us and someone is always just waiting to stymie our progress, especially when it comes to economic empowerment. Booker said, *We did not seek to give the people the idea that political rights were not valuable or necessary, but rather to impress upon them that economic efficiency was the foundation for every success.*

Another famous Washington quote, and there were many of them, regarding political involvement: *I do not believe the world ever takes a race seriously, in its desire to share in the government of a nation, until a large number of individual members of that race have demonstrated beyond question their ability to control and develop their own business enterprises.* Right again, Brother Booker.

To sum it all up, and in my own words, it's all about the money. We are still hung up on our political status and how many Black people we get into office. Yet we are unwilling to a great extent to put money into their campaigns. We want accountability but we do not want to pay for it. Well, the reality is that if we are going to play the political game we must be willing and able to pay the price of admission. An economic foundation would put us in the game and then some.

Once again, Booker says it best. *There are reports that in some sections the Black man has difficulty in voting and having counted the little white ballot he has the privilege of depositing twice a year. But there is a little green ballot he can vote through the teller's window 313 days each year and no one will throw it out or refuse to count it.* Enough said.

So what can we do when we leave this place to make Booker T's vision a reality again? The first thing we can do is to trust one another. If we do not learn to work together, to trust, to agree to disagree and still be friends and, more importantly, to pool our resources, Washington's "before it's too late" prediction will soon reverberate throughout our communities, across this nation, and around the world. We simply must change our minds about one another.

We must also take care of ourselves first. You know, even when we are in meetings with all Black people some of us are still talking about what we can do for "minorities." That way of thinking is what's keeping us down now. Our economic house is on fire and we are holding the ladder saying "after you" to everyone else. Does that make sense? I know we are a compassionate people, but give me a break!

We are in no position to help everybody else. As Flight Attendants instruct us, "If there is an oxygen deficiency in the cabin, put your mask on first and then assist someone else." There definitely is a deficiency among Black people, an economic deficiency, and it makes no sense for us to continue to allow others to call us minorities and treat us as though our history in this country is the same as every other group's. That only diffuses us even more, and it lessens our importance. We were here when the first hut was built in this country. There is no other group that holds the same status as Black Americans. If we don't acknowledge that, who will? Please do not allow yourself to be called a minority. Every other group in this country helps itself. We must do the same.

What we must do is what I discuss in my book. We have to change our minds. We must move from an unconscious state of economic incompetence, through the stages of conscious incompetence and conscious competence, to the ideal state of unconscious competence. Then, rather than a *chore*, it will be a *habit* for us to seek out Black businesses first when we spend our money. Trust, love, and sharing are what it takes.

In addition, in light of the growing class gap between the Black haves and the Black have-nots, those at the top must stop looking down their noses at their brothers and sisters at the bottom. They must come down from their lofty perches in business and academia and be willing to help our people.

Those at the bottom must stop the jealousy and the envy. They should learn to rejoice when a brother or sister does well. There is nothing wrong with making money—in this country it's all about money anyway. So let's not begrudge our own folks when they get some.

Those of us in the middle, where I consider myself, must be willing to lie down and be walked upon by those at the top and those at the bottom. Keep in mind that as they walk on us they get closer to one another. We become the much-needed bridges necessary to bring our people together again.

As for all of the rest of this country's citizens, many are worried about Black people getting together economically. Keep in mind that if Black people do well economically the entire country can't help but prosper. There is nothing wrong with self-interest. Every other group subscribes to that principle. Black people must do the same.

I will leave you with a poignant quote from Brother Booker T. Washington that points out how interdependent we are.

The laws of changeless justice bind
Oppressor with oppressed
And close as sin and suffering joined
We march to fate abreast

God bless you, thank you, and good night.

Happy Birthday, Marcus Garvey!

Because most of you who read my column already know a lot about Marcus Garvey, and because you know what he stood for and what he did, this will not be a history lesson. For those of you who are not as familiar with Brother Garvey as you would like to be, please go to a Black bookstore and get a few of the many books written about this giant.

No, this is not a history lesson. This is simply about homage, recognition, and allegiance to a Black man who loved his people so much that he sacrificed beyond what most of us would say is reasonable. This is about a man among men who told us to "rise up" and do the things we must do for ourselves to prosper in this country and around the world.

Marcus Garvey cared so much about his people that he kept coming back, even after being stymied and stigmatized by the white establishment as well as by some of his own people. After all of the negative experiences put upon him by his enemies, he kept coming back to fulfill his mission of raising the consciousness of Black people, organizing Black people, and leading Black people to economic prosperity. He even promised to come back in death as a whirlwind or a storm, bringing with him millions of Black slaves who would aid us in our fight for freedom and keep the pressure up until we have succeeded.

When you think about how hurricanes that come to the United States originate near the African coast, it makes you wonder if Brother Marcus is not fulfilling some of his prophecy. In addition, considering the latest flap over Firestone Tires, I wonder if Marcus is finally taking his retribution for that company's role in thwarting his work to link Blacks in the U.S. with our brothers and sisters in Liberia and West Africa via the UNIA. What goes around comes around. Right?

Marcus Garvey, yet another brother who departed this life much too soon—following Booker T. Washington's shortened life and preceding our dear brother and warrior, Amos Wilson - stood tall among all men. He was principled, he had backbone, and he was fearless—all because he loved his people dearly. Love is the most powerful weapon we have. If Black folks had "Marcus Love" for one another, imagine where we would be as a people.

Brother Garvey's life should be celebrated just as other icons of the Black experience are commemorated. After all, Garvey did what many of the others only talked about; he demonstrated the viability of economic control of our resources. Garvey showed our people how to pool our dollars and do for self; he carried us to new heights, collectively, by building numerous Black institutions and businesses.

Ironically, it was Brother Garvey's dedication to true nationalism that led to his demise among those for whom he so valiantly and relentlessly fought. Unfortunately some Blacks were jealous and envious of Marcus' ability to rally the people, to get Black people to raise huge sums of money, to march and demonstrate in overwhelming numbers, to turnout the vote in unprecedented fashion, and to deny the takeover of the UNIA by "outsiders." Black "leaders" of his time even came up with a "Marcus must go" campaign. Can you imagine that? I can. Anytime a strong Black man or Black woman stands up for our people, it is almost inevitable that another Black person will lead the charge against them.

Too often we forget, if we ever knew it at all, the importance of our brothers and sisters who stood tall on our behalf. Marcus Garvey, born August 17, 1887, is certainly deserving of our recognition and our honor. His words, *All I have I have given you*, are exemplary of this man's love for us. We should be proud of his accomplishments, and it would be wonderful if we would emulate his spirit, his love, and his tenacity as we make our way to economic freedom.

I will close with a portion of Marcus Garvey's letter from a prison in Atlanta. *I have sacrificed my home and my loving wife for you. I entrust her to your charge... I have left her penniless and helpless to face the world, because I gave all, but her courage is great, and I know she will hold up for you and me... After my enemies are satisfied, in life or death I shall come back to you to serve even as I have served before. In life I shall be the same; in death I shall be a terror to the foes of Negro liberty. If death has power, then count on me in death to be the real Marcus Garvey I would like to be. I may come in an earthquake, or a cyclone, or plague, or pestilence, or as God would have me, then be assured that I will never desert you and make your enemies triumph over you.*

Happy Birthday, Marcus Mosiah Garvey! We remember you. We honor you. We love you.

Thank you, Rosa Parks

...*I was tired of giving in.* Those were the words of the little lady we call the Mother of the Civil Rights Movement, Rosa Parks. Those words should be the mantra of Black people today as we celebrate the accomplishments of Rosa Parks and others like her.

Most of us know the story of Rosa Parks, but too few of us reflect on what she did and even fewer of us are willing to mimic her actions today. Her defiance in the face of overwhelming odds should suggest to us that we can overcome anything in our way. Her willingness to "do the right thing" and take a stand for her beliefs in 1955 should indicate to us quite graphically what our posture must be forty-five years later. Her solitary disobedience, shrouded from the public eye, without stage presence, and devoid of photo opportunities, should be a beacon that shows us the way to true freedom.

In our current world of selfish, self-centered, *what's-in-it-for-me* brothers and sisters, the Rosa Parks story should be plastered on every wall in every office and in every home. We should be forced to take a good hard look at what it means to take a position simply because we're tired of taking the inequity, the lack of reciprocity, the lack of respect, and the general unfairness doled out to Black people in this country.

While no one can do everything, everyone can do something. Rosa Parks was one person—alone. She was not surrounded by a support group, she did not have her "homeys" watching her back, and she was not seeking public attention when she refused to give up her seat. She did what she knew was right and took her stand based on principle, without knowing what would happen to her in return. Each of us can do the same if we choose the Rosa Parks' way.

The actions of this one lady turned the tide for civil rights for Black people in the United States. What can each of us, or any of us, do today to have that same impact?

Most assuredly times have changed, and our battle is no longer on the civil rights front. As Martin Luther King said, *The emergency we now face is economic.* So, how can one person in Y2K make the same kind of contribution Rosa Parks made in 1955? Well, you can simply decide that you will no longer accept disparate treatment, especially in return for the half-trillion dollar windfall Black people dump into this country's economy each year.

You can defy the odds by making your own personal commitment to withhold your dollars from those who disrespect you. Without fanfare or hoopla, you can refuse to give up your money, just like Rosa Parks refused to give up her seat. Like her, you can resolve to make a personal sacrifice for your people and for your own economic justice. You can "do your thing" in the marketplace and, guess what, you will not be arrested for your actions.

Rosa Parks was well aware of the rules of her day, but she was tired. We are aware of what is happening to our people economically. Are we tired enough to stop it? Rosa Parks was tired enough to say I will sit where I want on this bus. Are we tired enough to say, we will now own bus companies? That's what being tired in 2000 is all about. And, economically, we should be exhausted.

This year, as in years past, we will celebrate the strength and bravery of Rosa Parks and other giants in Black history. We will revel in their willingness to get out front and lay it on the line for their people. We will pay due homage to our *heroes and she-roes* for being role models and icons of "The Struggle." But, what will we do to truly honor them?

I think it would be appropriate for us to emulate them. I think Rosa Parks would beam with pride if she saw us working together to finish what she started—and it was simply a start, despite what some of our "leaders" would have us believe. I can see her beautiful smile now as she watches us on television cutting the ribbon to that new bus company. I can hear her laughing with joy as she hears on the radio that her people have opened a nationwide chain of hotels.

Oh yes, I can see Rosa Parks as she drifts off to sleep at night, comforted by the knowledge that her actions moved us beyond merely being able to sit in a certain seat on a bus or eat in a certain restaurant. I can see her patting us on our collective head and saying in her soothing reassuring voice, "I'm proud of you."

Wouldn't that be wonderful? So what's it going to be? Will you, just one person, and in Ms. Parks' reference to herself, "...just an average citizen," commit to doing whatever you can to move our people forward? Will you make just one defiant move, one radical gesture, one individual act that will let others know that you are just tired of giving in?

If each of us would do our part to resolve this "emergency we now face" there would be thousands of Rosa Parks in our midst. And like her, we would not only pay our fare, we would demand reciprocity—and settle for nothing less, regardless of the cost. The thousands of Rosa Parks would be the new economic army we desperately need to put an end, once and for all, to the economic exploitation we accept everyday.

The Rosa Parks army would answer its call to arms at the drop of a hat. It would marshal its forces and wage war on the robber barons of our time. It would not accept anything less than a plan for economic survival for Black people; and it would be more than willing to fight for it, to sacrifice for it, and to build it into the economic power we can be in this country.

This year and in years to come, let's make our "Mother" proud. She deserves no less.

Here's to You, Ida B. Wells

Long before Sister Rosa Parks did her thing, there was a diminutive but strong Black Sister named Ida B. Wells. In 1884, Ms. Wells refused to move from her seat in the "ladies" section of a train to one that was reserved for Negroes. Wells, who was referred to in the Memphis newspaper as the "Darkey Damsel," sued the train company and won, only to have her victory overturned by the state supreme court.

Nonetheless, Ida B. Wells, after enduring an horrendous childhood, losing both her parents—within twenty-four hours—and her youngest brother to yellow fever, went on to be one of the most feared journalists and bravest women in the history of this country.

We can and should take a lesson from this sister, not only for her courage under fire, but for her Black consciousness as well. She was unwilling to sell out, even if it meant losing her job as a schoolteacher, which she prized.

This gun-toting original "sister soldier" wielded a pen with the aplomb of any expert in the field of journalism. Her critics and supporters often suggested that were she a man she would have been elevated to an even higher plateau in society. Bravery and determination were her calling cards, and she truly understood how to use the power of the written word to the advantage of her people. Frederick Douglass spoke highly of Sister Wells, commending her for her bravery and tenacity, saying she had been of great service to her people and to him.

At fourteen, after her parents died, Ms. Wells took on the responsibility of caring and providing for her younger siblings, one of whom was crippled and could not care for herself. She took the test to be a schoolteacher and passed it right away. She later lost her job as a teacher for writing an article about the terrible conditions that existed in the Memphis Black public schools. Just as we see today, many of the "Negroes" at that time were afraid to support her position, and left her out there alone to fight by herself for their children, and Ida was fired.

That incident probably opened the door for the personality we read about today. Ida B. Wells was now able to devote all of her energies to writing. And, boy did she write! Her mission was to expose the hate-filled mobs that lynched Black people, to fill the pages of the press with the horror stories of white men, women, and children who took holidays to witness the maiming, torture, and murder of Blacks. She exposed the lies they told for their abominable acts by actually traveling to the cities where lynchings took place and interviewing eyewitnesses.

White news editors wrote scathing articles about Ms. Wells and her *exposes*, but to no avail. She was undeterred by their threats and continued to write. They even attempted to intimidate other Black people, trying to get them to "remedy" the problem of this "uppity Negress." I can see some of them, cowering and saying, *"Yes sah boss, you right. We needs to git rid a dis troublemaka."* (You know, there are Black folks who say that today, just without the plantation flavor.)

Angry whites finally resorted to their favorite tactic. They formed a mob and destroyed the Free Speech newspaper for which Ida wrote. Fortunately for some of them, and for Ida, the dastardly deed was done when Ida was away attending a meeting in New Jersey. Had she been there she probably would have shot a few of the mob and they probably would have killed her. She even said she thought they would resort to destroying the business, but she figured it would be when she was at home in Memphis. It was a good thing for some of them that they were cowards.

This pioneer later became Ida B. Wells-Barnett after she married Ferdinand Barnett, the founder of the first Black newspaper in Chicago, and went on to travel abroad and across this country spreading her fiery brand of journalism. She pulled the covers off liars and murderers and worked unceasingly for the rights of her people. She had tremendous Black pride, unlike many of us who only speak about it today, and she wore it proudly for all to see. In other words, she loved her people and never apologized for it. We should be so fortunate to have more Ida B. Wells among us today.

Another Black woman who refused to give up her seat on public transportation, Ida B. Wells-Barnett should be discussed, studied, and revered a great deal more by Black people—especially our children. They know Rosa P., but do they know Ida B.? Do you?

Understanding Our Problem

Understanding is a fountain of life to those who have it, but folly brings punishment to fools.
Proverbs 16:22

Ain't understanding mellow?
Jerry Butler and Brenda Lee Eager

This next series of articles deals with the nature of our people and our propensity to remain divided. It lays out stark examples of misguided actions toward one another as well as toward those who offend us. And it illustrates the position we are in as regards employment, consumption spending, disunity, and the squandering of our resources.

We have come to a point where it seems to be easier to complain about what we do not have rather than to celebrate and capitalize on the resources we do have. The psychology of a people who - despite our half trillion dollars - remain divided and non-supportive of one another is profoundly distressing.

Our problem begins with our psychological make-up. It is grounded in the programming we received many years ago. Our problem, while it can be solved, hangs around our collective neck like an albatross. Only we can remove it, and I hope we will.

The first thing we must do, as with any problem, is to understand it. Then we must accept the facts surrounding the problem. We must admit both our shortcomings and our strengths and resolve to do what we must to change our minds and our actions.

Black people can gain an understanding of the problem by looking squarely at our economic situation in this country and realizing that our economy is operating at a trade deficit. We must work to reduce that deficit through ownership, control of our resources, wealth retention, and mutual support. But, psychological freedom is the pre-requisite for all of those ideals. Let's move beyond meaning-less efforts and empty victories, and let's go get our freedom!

The Parable of the Talents – 1990's Style.

God gave Black people 500 billion talents. He gave Hispanic people 350 billion talents. He gave Asian people 225 billion talents. He left us alone for one year and then returned to see what we had done with our talents

God asked the Asian people, **"What have you done with your resources?"** The Asians replied, "We created many businesses and purchased many franchises. We used our resources to assist our families and our Asian friends, helping them to get into business as well."

The Asians continued, "Lord, we knew that with 225 billion talents we could generate even more talents by pooling what we had and working together toward a common economic goal. We have doubled the amount you awarded us. We now have 550 billion talents. And to top it all off, our restaurants are going strong; everybody loves our food!"

The Lord said, **"Well done, my good and faithful servants. I will make you rulers over many things."**

God then asked the Hispanic people what they had done with their inheritance. They gleefully replied, "Lord, You are really going to be proud of us. Upon receipt of our talents we went to work right away and formed our own bank. We have one in Florida that ranks among the largest in all the land. And You know what else? The interest we are making will more than double the amount of talents You gave us."

As God nodded approvingly, the Hispanic people couldn't wait to continue. "We opened fast food shops and sidewalk stands. We sold fruit, enchiladas, and tacos. We supported Hispanic doctors, lawyers, accountants, and all the Hispanic businesses we could find. If a certain business did not exist in our community, we pooled our resources and started new ones. We have done very well, Lord, especially considering the short time we have been in this land."

And God said, **"Well done, my good and faithful servants. I will make you rulers over many things."**

Since God had given the most talents to His chosen people—Black people—He couldn't wait to hear what they had done with their 500 billion talents. Like a doting father, He proudly asked them, **"What have you done with your inheritance?"**

After turning their music down in order to hear what God was saying, the Black people waved their hands in the air (like they just didn't care) and shouted, "Lord, we just threw the party of the century, and it was all good! Look at those *bad rides* parked outside. We bought them from the German people and the Japanese people. Wouldn't You agree, Lord, that we did good deeds by helping to make them wealthy?"

Even God looked perplexed. He asked if there was anything else the Black people wanted to report. "Oh yeah," they replied. "You haven't heard the half of it, Lord. We're the most charitable people on earth. We spent 95% of all You gave us with businesses other than our own. We helped everyone. We didn't discriminate and we didn't playa-hate."

Then one of the Black leaders spoke up. "You know how we like nice clothes, Lord. So after the party we went out and bought all of the latest styles with all of the right labels. You know what I'm saying? We just had to have it; we couldn't wait. Check us out."

Now the Lord was quite concerned about His people and their attitude regarding their talents. Continuing to probe and expecting to hear something that would make Him proud, God pleaded, **"Surely you have done something with your inheritance to generate more talents for yourselves?"**

The Black people looked around at one another, and one of their "leaders" stepped forward to sum things up. "Lord, we have the finest cars, we eat and drink only top shelf, and we meet in the most elaborate hotels. Our children have several pairs of the latest gym shoes, we make the *baddest* videos and we can throw down—I mean dance—with the best of them. Even better than that, we have good jobs to earn back our 500 billion talents next year, and we will again be able to help all the other inhabitants of this land."

Sadly, God looked at His people and said, **"With what you have done with your talents, you may as well have buried them in the ground. Because of your slothfulness and lack of good stewardship, I will give your future talents to those who have the least. You have gravely disappointed me by not adhering to one of my most important admonishments:** To whom much is given, much is expected."

Calling it as I See it

My article in the July-August (1999) issue of *African American Magazine* titled, **Majoring in the Minors**, describes the ever-increasing waste of time—precious time—by our people when it comes to concentrating on our differences rather than on what we have in common.

Well, if you look closely you will see that we are wasting even more time complaining, protesting, seeking apologies, and "supposedly" boycotting for what we perceive as economic and social transgressions against Black people in this country. We say we want economic empowerment but our actions indicate something entirely different.

Let's take a look. Currently we have been asked to seek apologies and other forms of retribution from a Senator in Colorado, two disc jockeys, a giant media company, a computer outlet, another oil company, a confederate flag, the big four television networks, and a major soft drink company, although no one seems to want to follow through on the soft drink company.

What are we attempting to achieve by our actions, as unorganized as they may be? Well, some of us want money (wouldn't you guess) for our pain and suffering. Some of us want those mean people to apologize for calling us those bad names. Others would like to see more Black people on television and in the movies. And some want more jobs, more promotions of Black people, more media buys, more advertising, and the one I cannot understand, more acknowledgment for the purchasing habits of Black people. In other words, we want them to "recognize"—as our young people say.

To borrow another term from our young people, we had better start to "represent." Instead of getting bogged down with issues that only lead to a few Black people getting paid, or resulting in us having the luxury of seeing ourselves on television a little more (we need to watch less TV anyway—maybe the lack of Blacks on screen is a good thing), we should "represent" by doing our own thing.

61

If we are truly interested in economic empowerment, why are we spending so much time on such superficial issues, especially if winning our fights on those issues does not lead us to our ultimate goal? The Urban League, the NAACP, Black Chambers of Commerce, National Business Leagues, hundreds of Black churches and other organizations all say their number one agenda item is economic empowerment. Are they (are we?) following through on that agenda item the way they should be? Or, are we wasting a lot of precious time trying to get over individually?

If we are really serious we should be getting together, pooling our tremendous resources, and building our own economic infrastructure. We should be working to capture particular niches in the marketplace, just like a certain group from India has done in the motel industry of this country. The last time I checked they controlled 67% of that industry.

We put out report cards on telephone carriers and hotels and issue "white papers" (what a title) on companies that are discriminating against Black people, but we are not spending much time purchasing our own telecommunications networks. We are not establishing capital funds to purchase a few of those hotels that do us wrong. We seldom follow through on these so-called boycotts, and if we do boycott, while we are withdrawing our dollars from some business, wouldn't it be a nice idea if we set those dollars aside for ourselves? No, instead we simply take the money and give it to some other business.

It makes no sense for us to boycott anyone if we are simply going to return to them after they dip into their *"caught-in-the-act-contingency-fund"* to pay a few of us off. It does nothing for our collective economic empowerment if we spend our time seeking apologies from bigots, insisting that racists take sensitivity training, having national forums on certain flags being flown, trying to prove how much money we spend on certain products (believe me, they already know anyway), or trying to hurt someone rather than helping ourselves.

If we continue down the road we are on, which is merely saber-rattling, "talking loud and saying nothing" as the Godfather of Soul said, our economic demise will soon be sealed. Our window of opportunity is closing fast. We must begin to "seek for ourselves" as Absalom Jones, Peter Williams, and Richard Allen said when they formed the A.M.E. Church. Enough with empty meaningless threats. Enough of the superficial. On to the pragmatic. Black people need something concrete to assure and sustain the economic future of our children.

We do not need payoffs, temporary feel-good solutions, people saying they didn't mean what they said about us, placating tokenism by corporations (I thought we had enough of that in 1960's), or a few more jobs for a few more Black people, only to be laid off after things quiet down.

What we must do is make some sacrifices for ourselves and build our own economy. We must be willing to bring our organizations together to do what others do in this country—take care of our own. We must be capable of putting our super egos aside. It's not about one person, or even a small group of persons. Economic empowerment for Black people is not a solo act; it's a mass choir; it's a symphony orchestra. If one player cannot perform, the rest of us will make up the difference. The entire orchestra gets paid, not just the conductor.

We must stop these pseudo-movements in which we always seem to be entrenched. Can you imagine the conversations in that soft drink company accused of discrimination against Black people as we began buying even more of their product to collect their bottle caps? They must be laughing their heads off at us.

The flag issue. Who is the boycott hurting the most? Black vendors who make their living selling to South Carolina tourists? I sure would like to hear their opinion on this issue. If they say boycott, I am all for it. Sure, I understand boycotts will hurt some Blacks, but my concern is that it should also help Blacks at the same time. What if they capitulate and take the flag down? Will it be business as usual then? Will Black people simply go back to the same economic status we had before the boycott? If we institute an economic boycott, we should at least get some **collective** economic benefit from it. Black people in South Carolina will be the ones suffering; they should be the ones to benefit.

Apologies? Who needs them? Transgressors can and will say anything when they get caught. What is that worth to us? So we get some more jobs. If we don't change our ways, all that does is give us more money to spend with someone else, thus creating even more wealth for them.

I hope we come to realize the error of our ways and those of our so-called leaders. We are going nowhere fast. If we are going to advance our cause and move forward we have to do for ourselves, with ourselves, among ourselves. Black people must pool our resources and build our own institutions and businesses and stop seeking refuge in the superficial trappings of empty victories.

And Black people must learn to rely on one another, especially before we seek the favor of someone else. How many computers are purchased from Black computer companies by Black people? How much money do Black people spend with Black media? How many Black people are hired by Black owned companies? How many Black people are we asking to apologize for calling our women "B's" and "H's?" These are the questions we must answer. And we must change the results if they are not in the affirmative.

I say these things because I am tired of seeing our people—our children—move further and further down the economic ladder. I say these things because I love my people. So please, don't spend your time trying to assign some political slant to this message. It's not about Democrat or Republican. It's not about Conservative or Liberal. Those classifications do not interest me. It's about a "race first" philosophy and practice. If we concentrated on our own more, we would hardly have time to even notice when someone calls us a name.

To draw once again upon the wisdom of the Godfather, James Brown, he also said, *Let's get together and get some land; raise our food like the man; save our money like the mob; put up a factory, own the job.* You tell 'em, Godfather.

Aristocracy and Pauperism on the Rise

I am reminded of the fate of the infamous French Aristocracy, and its "Let them eat cake" philosophy, when I ponder our current economic situation. Wealth abounded in a few French families, but most other families suffered in abject poverty. Is this what the United States of America is becoming?

Robert Reich, former U.S. Secretary of Labor, referred to this new fashion of CEO's making million dollar windfalls after laying off thousands of workers, as *The disappearance of the implicit social contract that used to bind companies with their workers and communities.*

If he was correct, African Americans, especially, are in for a rough ride. We will get attacked from all directions. Downsize government (most affluent Black people have government jobs); downsize corporations (you know who goes first); privatize the public sector (who will get the lion's share of the contracts?); eliminate affirmative action (do you really know what a "colorblind" society will mean for us?); and, build more jails (who fills them now?).

Change is here, right before our eyes. How are we reacting to that change? Are we sitting back and buying the rhetoric coming out of Washington regarding the economy, jobs, taxes, welfare, and education? Are we being lulled to sleep by the "do-gooders" who would have us believe that everything will be all right if we simply continue to let "them" take care of us?

I sincerely hope not. If we want jobs we have to help make some jobs. If we want charity, we must first be willing to be charitable ourselves, and if we want to be educated we must open our own minds first. Corporate America is not the answer for the majority of us, and we must not look to it or the government to solve our problems. They simply do not care about us. Bottom line. The important thing, how ever, is how much **we** care about **us**.

Doesn't it make sense that the best way to eliminate the welfare system is to create more jobs rather than wiping them out by the thousands? Obviously the private sector is not interested in job creation, which leaves our good friend, the U.S. Government, the largest employer of higher income Black people. But wait, they want to downsize those jobs too. And then there are tax breaks; tax breaks don't mean a thing, if you don't have a job.

So whom are they kidding? They don't want us to share theirs, and they don't want us to build our own economic systems. What are we supposed to do? I'll tell you. Forget about them and worry about us. Create and nurture genuine **UNITY** in our communities. Pool our resources and create our own businesses. And while we are doing that, we must stop our feeding frenzy at everybody else's trough.

The United States is rapidly becoming a two-tiered society. You either have something or you do not. On which tier will we find ourselves in the next few years? When you think about it—I mean really think about it—it's frightening, especially when you add our children into the equation. What are we going to leave for them?

Jobs are very important, don't get me wrong. However, who controls those jobs is even more important. I once heard a man say he'd rather control a million dollars than to have a million dollars. Power is the ultimate aphrodisiac in this country. We had better be about getting and retaining some of it for ourselves.

Stop the bickering. Stop the hatred. Stop the jealousy. Stop the selling out. Stop the back-biting.

Start trusting. Start loving. Start helping. Start building.

Economic self-sufficiency is the only way we will move forward in this country—this capitalistic society, in which Black people cannot hope to eat cake. Crumbs will be the only item on our menu if we do not change our minds toward one another.

Are You Feeling Good or Doing Good?

Brothers and sisters, we must get down to real business. For too long we have been engulfed in a sea of emotionalism, riding on a wave of ecstasy, and drowning in our own "feel good" approach to economically empowering ourselves. Some of us are so steeped in the emotional messages we hear everyday that we forget, if we recognized it at all, the message of collective economic redemption and what it will take for us to achieve it.

We see it so often. We will pay tremendous amounts of money to be uplifted for a little while by someone who tells us we are all winners. We pack the house when someone is in town discussing how each of us can "make it big." We hold in the highest esteem those who bring virtually nothing to the table, regarding Black cooperative economics, and pay them dearly for their time.

But bring in a brother or a sister who has a message or a plan for our people to escape the chains of economic deprivation, and watch us scatter. Watch us find something else to do.

Have you ever wondered why many of us are so enthralled by emotion-laden messages? Have you noticed how difficult it is to get some of our people aroused when it comes to messages that require critical thinking, research, or action?

Emotion is a wonderful thing; don't get me wrong. I love to be entertained; I love to be swept away emotionally. But we cannot allow our mere emotions to control our everyday actions or the lack of appropriate actions when it comes to our economic survival. You must admit that we are "in the house" when entertainers come to our cities. We will pay whatever the price to see them, go through all kinds of weather (Why won't we do that when it comes to voting?) postpone or cancel anything else in conflict with the event, and rise to a fever pitch while we are being entertained.

Our emotions are stirred tremendously by motivational speakers. They make us look into ourselves and realize our potential, at least for the moment. They rally the winner in all of us and cause us to commit, for the moment, to do better, to work harder, to make more money, and to "win" in the game of life.

On Sunday mornings millions of Black people are stimulated emotionally, and their religious fervor is such that we make promises, new commitments, and declarations to God Himself. We sing, dance, cry, testify, and issue prayers and supplications proclaiming our new being and how we are going to change the way we have lived.

With all of these emotional outlets and emotional experiences available to Black people you would think we would be the most active people on the face of the earth. You would think we would have, by now, gained all of the benefits and prosperity we so often speak about in our emotional sessions. You would think that by now we would have transposed some of our emotion into work—work that will lead us to economic freedom. You would think.

As we continue to expend enormous energy on emotional activities, and we will continue it, let's make a conscious and concerted effort to parlay that emotion into something pragmatic and tangible. After we are entertained, let's at least ask: "Who received the lion's share of the proceeds and what are they doing with it?" After we have heard the motivational speeches, many of which we paid so dearly to hear, let's go out and follow through on what we have heard and make our lives better. And after the soul-stirring sermons we hear each Sunday, or any other day, let's go home and get to work being more loving, more trusting, kinder, and fairer to one another as a people.

Finally, if you really want to "do" good rather than merely "feel" good, get in the freedom business. Economic freedom is the greatest cause before Black people today. Similar words were spoken by the President of the National Negro Business League in 1950, Mr. Horace Sudduth. His words still apply, and if we want true economic freedom we must do more than make emotional speeches. We must do more than come up with schemes and scams that only put a sour taste in our mouths. And, we must do much more than rally, march, protest, complain, whine, seek apologies, and turn over our tremendous wealth to other folks' businesses.

We must do for ourselves, with the resolve and the willingness to sacrifice for one another, if we are going to attain true economic freedom. It's much more than just feeling good for a little while and going home. It's about exchanging our dollars, pooling our resources, and building our own communities. Yes, we can go to the concerts, listen to the motivational speeches, and pay close attention to the sermons. But follow through is everything. Oh yes, let's also try packing the house when someone is making a presentation on how to get our economic freedom.

I ask you: Are you feeling good and then doing good? Or, are you just feeling good?

Majoring in the Minors

Quite often we find ourselves embroiled in a skirmish in which, at the end of the day, even if we win, our net gain is absolutely nothing. Many times we get involved in matters that turn out to be mere diversions from what is really important to our people—and what really is important is economics. Of course there are other issues facing us everyday, but as Booker T. Washington told us, *At the bottom of politics, at the bottom of education, even at the bottom of religion, lies economics.*

I don't know about you and your situation but I think it's a pretty good bet that, no matter where you live in this country, there are heated discussions on things like what we should call ourselves (Black, African American, African, etc.), what we should wear (didn't we go through that one in the 1960's?), and "Robots' Rules of Order" in our meetings (some call them Roberts' Rules).

These issues provoke deep emotional conversations and more often than not lead to our people withdrawing from one another rather than moving closer together as we should be doing. These issues, among the many others we get caught up in, tend to keep us from our charge of uplifting our people collectively.

The most important issue facing Black (or African or African American) people today is economics. Horace Sudduth, as President of the National Negro Business League, uttered those words in 1951. Think about it. Black businesses were doing pretty well back then, comparatively speaking. If he and others felt then that economics was the top issue, what should our thoughts be today? A better question is: What should our actions be today?

Rather than spending our valuable time beating up one another about names, titles, positions, and points-of-order we should be building our trust in and love for one another. Rather than worry so much about the traditional differences that have been laid before us such as light skin versus dark skin, straight hair versus curly, Baptist versus

Methodist, Mercedes versus Chevrolet, Democrat versus Republican, mansion versus shotgun house, and all the other silly things that plague our people, let's get down to real business.

If economics is the most important issue facing us today, then we must act upon that fact – not just discuss it ad nauseam. We must put aside our petty differences and throw off our cloaks of divisiveness, and we must be about the business of leaving a positive economic legacy for our children—NOW. If it was critical in 1951 and critical in 1900 and critical in 1867, it must surely be absolutely critical to us in this new millennium.

Our charge from people like Washington, Bethune, Garvey, Douglass, Malcolm, King, and all the rest is to take up the economic gauntlet and move our people forward. We reminisce and brag about the good old days of the Greenwood District in Tulsa, Oklahoma; we remember the all-Black towns and the economic foundations built by our people; we daydream about the days when Black people worked together in support of one another; and we long for the times when we used to take care of our own.

Well, it's time to wake up. Stop dreaming and remin-iscing and start doing something to reconstruct the economic legacy our grandparents and great-grandparents left us. Stop majoring in the minors. Stop being so intellectual and so above it all that we miss what is really important. Start thinking of ourselves as a nation within a nation, because after all is said and done, no matter how far up the ladder you go or how "accepted" you feel you are, you are still Black or African or whatever you want to call yourself.

Other groups practice nationalism everyday, and they prosper by doing so. Why shouldn't we do it? There's absolutely nothing wrong with it. Somehow we have been programmed to believe that doing for self and putting our people first is wrong, but unless we begin practicing a nationalistic approach to economically empowering our people we will continue to find ourselves in the same position we fight against daily.

Let's get our priorities in line. Let's understand that our economic position in this country can be determined by what we do—together. Of course we are not going to accomplish everything in a year or two—or even a decade or two. It will take quite some time, but isn't it worth it? Isn't our economic future and that of our children worth putting aside the "minors?" Our first priority must be economics because that's what runs this country, and unless we are planning a mass exit we had better get into the game.

So what's next? Stop bickering about meaningless things. We don't have the time to do that. Start trusting and loving one another enough to share our intellectual and financial resources Stop thinking scarcity and start thinking abundance. This is not a zero-sum game we are playing. There is plenty to go around. In order to capture our share we must work together as other groups do.

Stop the crime against our own people. Start policing ourselves and incorporate what the brothers at the Black Library in Chicago taught back in 1970, Black Law. We can and should deal with our own people through a code of conduct that if broken will lead to serious sanctions. If we don't police our own, the police will continue to do it, and you know what their answers are. Kill us or put us in jail.

As one brother said during my recent radio interview in Inglewood, California, "We know what the problems are, what we need are solutions." I say, we even know what the solutions are, what we need to do is act upon those solutions. Stop majoring in the minors. Our major must be in economics, more specifically economic empowerment. Enroll in a class near you and don't be a dropout. Even better, make the Honor Roll.

Section Three

This "Question" of Unity

In the next century, ... global tribes will play an ever more important role in the emerging world economy.
Joel Kotkin

Can't...can't we all just get along?
Rodney King

Now here is a word that is probably the most over-used one in the Black lexicon: Unity. Have you ever heard a word used so much and not see the action required to bring the concept to fruition?

Why is it so hard to bring about the unity we so often shout out to one another? Do we really mean what we say or do we merely love to hear ourselves talk? Are we ready for unity? Can we achieve it?

I think we can, but only to the extent that we understand what it really means to us as a people. In addition, we must understand and accept the fact that not all Black people want unity and will not participate in unifying efforts. That's why the title of this section characterizes "unity" as an interrogatory concept.

This section addresses various forms of unity among Black people. One of my favorite pieces is ***Economic Symphony***. It suggests that each of us has a part to play and if we play those parts together, in support of one another, we will make beautiful music together and we will win our economic battle. It stresses *harmonic unity*.

This section also discusses other efforts involving unity, such as standing together and leveraging the power we possess as Black people. If we truly want unity, all we need to do is practice it. If we want unity we must be willing to subordinate our individual agenda in deference to our collective agenda. Sure, we can and must seek our own individual calling and outcome, but we must also seek a collective and cooperative outcome for our people.

Yes, this notion of Black unity seems to be an oxymoron in some circles, but there is movement within various organizations to change that. I have hope and trust that we will achieve the level of unity we need to establish a firm economic foundation for our children. What do you think? A better question: What are you going to do to help?

The Power of the People

Back in the good old days known as the 60's, we shouted "Power to the People." We raised our fists in anger and defiance, and were determined to show the establishment that we meant business—that we would take the power we sought *by any means necessary*. Black brothers and sisters moved in unison toward our common goal: Power.

While it was a noble cause, as we assess our situation today we still see a huge void when it comes to Black power. What did we mean by *power*? What were we trying to capture? What gains were we seeking? Voting rights? Fair housing? Right to work? Equal education? Equality in general? All of those things were mentioned more than once during those days, but very few times did we hear screams for economic power.

These days we find ourselves trying to "catch up." The power we should have begun to work for, just after we won our "civil rights," is economic power. Now we have coined new phrases such as the "third movement," the "new civil rights movement," the "last frontier," and the "last great hurdle." Economic power has become the catchphrase of the 90's. And to tell you the truth, I love it.

I want us to take whatever phrase we'd like to use and capitalize on it until we have reached an economic plateau that is commensurate not only with our population and income but also our responsibility and obligation to one another. I want our people to adopt the fourth principle of Kwanzaa as our mantra—and act upon it. Time out for the usual emotionalism and the temporary support within our ranks. This time, let's do it.

All of the principles of Kwanzaa are important, but it is likely that if we do not seek and conquer Ujamaa first, the rest of them will be more difficult to achieve and sustain. The power we now seek is contingent upon the degree to which we are able to cooperate with one another economically. Our very survival in this country depends upon our ability and willingness to form alliances, partnerships, and cooperatives among our businesses and with the businesses of others.

Our continued viability hinges on our commitment to share our financial resources as well as our intellectual resources. Our true power lies in our action, not our rhetoric. We must throw off the old ways and adopt new strategies for our economic security. We need to move quickly to bridge the widening class-gap we see among Black people if we truly desire this power we seek.

The power of the people rests in our hands, in our minds, and in our souls. All we have to do is grab hold to it and refuse to let go. Use our tremendous financial resources for the benefit of as many Black people as possible. Stop succumbing to the commercial pitfalls and traps that lie before us in the marketplace of this country. Deny our dollars to those that hold us in disdain and do not reciprocate for our patronage of their businesses. Change the "I got mine, you get yours" attitudes; adopt an "I got mine, now let me go back and help get someone else get theirs" attitude.

The power of our people can be found in our pockets and purses. If we continue to give it away, we will sentence our children to the same empty strategy many of us used – just talking loud and doing nothing. But if we change our minds about one another and practice Ujamaa everyday of the year rather than celebrate it one day per year, we will surely be successful.

That's what economic power is all about, and that's what it will take for us to achieve it. Are you ready? On your mark, get set, GO!

An Economic Symphony

In addition to the sounds emanating from an orchestra, one of my favorite things is to watch the members of the orchestra. I observe each individual and I look at the different musical units, especially the violins and cellos. You know what amazes me? Each of the string players' hands—their movements are all exactly alike. They all make the same strokes of their bows at exactly the same time, in the same direction, and in the same area of the strings. Their fingers move up and down the strings precisely and in unison.

I know they practice this. I know someone composed the music and they are simply reading it together as they play. Still, it amazes me to see that kind of cooperation, that kind of collaboration, and that kind of strict discipline among so many individuals. Now throw in the horns, the reeds, the drums, the harp, and keyboards, each group or individual playing a certain pattern of notes, and you really have something to behold. The sound is fantastic. Everyone knows his or her part and plays it perfectly, without jealousy or resentment of the other. They play without trying to upstage the other. They play cooperatively, in support of one another—and the music they make is utterly beautiful.

Black people could follow that example by making our own brand of economic music. We would call it our economic symphony orchestra. Can you imagine the beautiful harmonious sounds of Black people working together in support of one another? Wouldn't it be great to compose our own music for a change? Wouldn't it be wonderful for a million Black people, all playing from the same sheet music, to move in unison toward the common goal of giving a command performance on the world's stage?

I can see it now. The maestro (or maestros) raises his or her baton to begin the performance. All of the players are prepared and well rehearsed. Each one knows his or her individual parts. The audience waits with pitched anticipation for the show to begin. The first sound we hear is a booming resonation similar to the beginning of Beethoven's Fifth Symphony. The concert has begun.

The director motions for the violins, the lead group, to do the opening—to explain our economic strategy. These are the local organizers, the Black Chambers of Commerce, the Black Business Leagues, and other economic empowering organizations. The maestro then brings in the French Horns, the community organizers, to sound the alarm among the masses. They continuously encourage us to create wealth by developing new businesses and supporting those we already have. They promote responsibility and integrity among our business owners toward their consumers.

The cellos, our elders, play a back-up role to the violins, reiterating the message at a slow gentle pace. The reed section, our teachers and professors, make a smooth transition of the economic message and pass it on to the trumpets, our youth.

Loudly and boisterously, our young people play their parts with verve, and it becomes just as important to them as rap music. As a matter of fact, they begin to compose their own brand of economic empowerment rap music!

By this time everyone is playing. The string bass and the drums, our ministers, are strumming and pounding out the timing pattern maintaining our focus on our mission. Oboes and bassoons, our unsung heroes and "she-roes" who work hard but get little attention, are steadily doing their thing. The audience has to really concentrate to hear them, but believe me they are there.

The trombones and tubas, our strong fathers, are belting out directions, taking their proper places in leading their families. The harps, our mothers, provide the beautiful melodies, soothing to our ears but yet strong, supporting, encouraging, and urging us to go on—to play our music louder—to move to new heights. The flutes and piccolos, our beautiful children, merrily play their parts, dashing in and out but gaining more knowledge of their roles each passing moment.

Our economic symphony has indeed begun and is a rousing success. We get a standing ovation and set out on a world tour that will run for the next fifty years. We play our music without malice toward one another, we play without being jealous of who is getting a lead solo, and we play without envy and without emphasis on our own individual accomplishments. We play with the understanding that if each of us plays our part well, we will all be successful.

The Black people's economic symphony is coming to your city. Make plans to take up your instrument and play your part. You may not think you can play well enough to be in the orchestra, but understand that the larger the orchestra the more accommodating it can be toward the less talented. Those who have more talent will cover for those of us who are less talented.

Plan to play for as long as you are physically able to do so. When the going gets tough, you might move from one of the heavier, more difficult, instruments to an easier one, but keep on playing, please. Don't stop until you hear the sound of the mighty cymbals.

If we play our parts in this economic symphony, it will be a hit. It will be the talk of the town. It will lead us to true economic empowerment. That's music to my ears.

Standing Together

Having written a great deal about the latent power of Black athletes, especially those who participate in football and basketball, I see the current situation in the National Basketball Association as good news and bad news.

Let me give you the bad news first. I miss Michael Jordan. Man, do I miss him! I miss the Bulls. It looks like I will also miss the annual Christmas duel between Chicago and New York. It is quite possible that I will not see one single NBA game this season. And the worst thought is that I may never again see MJ "do his thing." But it had to end one day, right? And even he cannot top what could be the final play of his illustrious career. At least I don't think so. But he is Michael, so I'd better retract that statement.

Here's the good news. For years I have posited that if our Black athletes would ever get together and stick together they could control the destiny of their respective sports. That day has finally come. Of course, there are some players who are not as well off as others and some that will be hurt by their action. But most things that are worth fighting for are also worth the sacrifice that must be made for their accomplishment. What is important is the way the players are looking out for one another and trying to help their peers financially.

The collective and unwavering stance made by the players of the NBA must be held up as an economic empowering strategy worthy of emulation throughout Black America. Yes, these are multi-millionaires who can afford not to work for a while, but keep in mind that everything is relative. The more we earn, the more we spend, even if it is on the ridiculous, such as ten automobiles and the like.

The overriding lessons in what took place were cooperation and tenacity. These brothers were determined to hold their line for the long haul. They were willing to lose untold sums of money for what they believed was right. They took a stand for economic justice. The players were in a high stakes poker game with the owners, and the first one to blink lost. Would they compromise? My guess was that as they got closer to January, when most of the NBA games were televised, some kind of concession would be reached. Just imagine how much the owners stood to lose when the real season began.

But I digress. I want to commend those players for demonstrating to the rest of us what unity is all about. I saw no one breaking rank, no one bad-mouthing the leadership, and no one sneaking in the back door trying to cut an individual deal. Black and white players were making a statement, but it's the Black players who were providing the lesson to the rest of the brothers and sisters—an important lesson in economic empowerment.

That lesson is not about how much money you have; it's about how much commitment you have. The lesson is not found at the sacred altar of sports; you will find it in your neighborhoods, in your corner stores, in your malls, and at the local theaters. The lesson the NBA players are teaching us, translated to the way we do business and spend our half-trillion dollars each year, if followed, would solve a major problem for Black people. If we work together, even though we are not all equal in status, we can have the kind of impact that will move us forward economically.

If we stand together, unwavering in our resolve, we can develop the economic infrastructure necessary for building our communities and establishing our economic self-sufficiency. If we put the world on notice once and for all that we will no longer accept or acquiesce to the economic exploitation of our race, we will be respected—maybe resented, but surely respected. If we tear down the walls that separate us, economically, socially, religiously, educationally, and psychologically, and take our places alongside one another, what a powerful force we will be.

While I hope the NBA solves its problems, I was proud to see these brothers stand tall and straight. I hope and trust they will not lose their will to persevere and never allow the flame of their unity to be extinguished. More importantly, I hope we will not lose the lesson taught by the players of the NBA. We need all the lessons we can get on economic empowerment—and learning to stand and stay together is lesson number one.

Section Four

This "Question" of Leadership

There are two types of leaders: those who protest and those who lead by taking action and building institutions.
Floyd Flake

Negroes... sometimes choose their own leaders but unfortunately they are too often of the wrong kind. Negroes do not readily follow persons with constructive programs.
Carter G. Woodson

This is one of my favorite topics. Black leadership has been and continues to be a paradox. On one hand we have thousands of leaders. Each year in virtually every city, Black leadership classes convene and graduate new "leaders." In my hometown we have Black "leaders" tripping over one another. Of course many of those so-called leaders have been ordained by the white establishment, which causes some of them to think they are better than those they are supposed to lead. But that's another subject.

On the other hand, we have problems that have plagued Black people for years and continue to hold us back year after year. Again, in my hometown, we experience the same kinds of problems each year and cannot seem to do anything to solve them—despite having so many Black "leaders" in our midst. Something is wrong with this picture, and it duplicates itself all over this country.

Thus, the "question" of leadership. Do we have true leaders? Where are they leading us? Is anyone following them? Are our leaders concerned about us or themselves? Are our leaders selling us out to the highest bidder? What exactly is leadership anyway?

I love Carter G. Woodson's discussion of leadership. In his timeless work, **The Mis-Education of the Negro**, Dr. Woodson posits, *The race needs workers, not leaders.* He goes on to say, *If the Negro could abandon the idea of leadership and instead stimulate a larger number of the race to take up definite tasks and sacrifice their time and energy in doing these things efficiently the race might accomplish something.*

In other words, true leaders are servants. Who are you following and what are they doing? Just leading, or serving?

More words from Brother Woodson. *Under leadership we have come into the ghetto; by service within the ranks we*

83

may work our way out of it. Under leadership we have been constrained to do the biddings of others; by service we may work out a program in the light of our own circumstances. Under leadership we have become poverty-stricken; by service we may teach the masses how to earn a living honestly. Under leadership we have been made to despise our own possibilities and to develop into parasites; by service we may prove sufficient unto the task of self-development and contribute our part to modern culture.

Who am I to think I can add anything to the words of this intellectual Elder? I rest my case.

Economic Leadership

During the 1950's and 1960's leaders of the civil rights movement rallied other individuals and trained them to carry out the strategies and tactics necessary to win the war they were waging.   These leaders had the expertise and the tenacity to begin the long march that lay before them. They had the strength, the will, the intellectual resources, and they took the initiative by getting out front on the issue.   They were willing to make the sacrifices necessary for their future generations to have the same rights as everyone else in this country. In other words, they were willing to serve as well as lead.

True leaders are servants. They are willing to get into the battle rather than direct it; they inspire their followers by the sacrifices they make; and they do what is necessary to win the fight, not just talk about it. It's sad to say, considering the economic resources Black people have today, that our economic leadership is unwilling to serve by making sacrifices, by getting into the fight, by speaking out, and by taking the initiative to rally the rest of us to the number one imperative.

It's also sad that those of our people who have the greatest financial resources are not at the head of the line, leading the way to economic freedom. Instead, many of them are wrapped up in the socialite world, in political circles, and are too busy promoting themselves to spend a little time promoting economic empowerment for Black people. And others seem to be more interested in assimilation and being seen with the "right folks" than to take a moment to make a public statement on behalf of their own people, not to mention doing something on their behalf.

Can you imagine the results of our top business people, our richest entertainers, our super-rich athletes, and our "mega-church" ministers getting together at an economic summit to develop a strategy for the economic uplift of their Black brothers and sisters? That would be powerful. I know we have already seen individual Black

85

moguls getting together to do their deals, but I am talking about a collective effort comprising hundreds of our people.

Their subject would be economic empowerment. Their goal would be to work together, with their resources, to maximize and centralize their dollar power for the benefit of their people. For instance, they would plan to establish new businesses in manufacturing and distribution, to purchase land, to buy hotels and banks, to start investment funds, to establish new schools, and then rally the rest of us to their support. In other words, they would serve and they would lead.

They would demonstrate their willingness to dedicate a portion of their tremendous wealth and influence to the uplift of Black people. They would define for us an economic movement, the likes of which have never been executed in the history of Black people in this country.

These Black people, the richest ever, with billions of dollars, could change the economic landscape of this nation if they so desired. They would not have to give up their primary causes, their affiliations and friendships, their ability to obtain more financial resources, their status in the white community, nor compromise their principles. That's the value of working together. The collective strength of the richest among us doing anything together is mind-boggling and could not be stopped. They would have the ability to reward their friends and punish their enemies. That's power.

I am told that some of our affluent Black public icons are afraid to get too close to Black people and Black causes such as economic empowerment because they think they will lose their sphere of influence in the dominant community. When I ask why certain Black people will not speak up on economic issues and step up to help solve problems, I am told they are fearful of being perceived as "too Black." I guess O.J. Simpson had the same fear, but when he found himself in trouble, where did he run? That's right. He came running to his Black brothers and sisters for refuge. Prior to his troubles he was too busy *assimilatin'* and "transcending race."

All I am asking is for us to do what every other group in this country does. It's not a crime, it's not a sin, and it's not a social *faux pas* to care about your own people and to help them as much as you can. We can be friends with whomever we want, but we must not feel compelled to distance ourselves from one another because of what we think our friends will say about us. Besides, if they are true friends, they will understand, respect, and support our decisions.

Where are our economic servants? Where are our economic leaders? I say they are in the office buildings, in the sports arenas (and on the golf courses), on television, in the pulpits, and on the silver screens. There is an army of foot soldiers awaiting their call to arms. All they need to do is say the word. I know I will be there. How about you?

Is it Safe?

With many of our "Leaders" finally jumping on Booker T. Washington's and Marcus Garvey's economic bandwagon now, I think back to a movie titled, "Marathon Man." The particular scene that comes to mind is the one in which Dustin Hoffman was about to be tortured with dental instruments by Laurence Olivier, who kept repeating, "Is it safe?"

This is a question that I am sure some of our leaders have been asking for quite some time. Now, some thirty-five years after MLK was assassinated while fighting for an economic cause, our leaders have apparently answered that question with a resounding "Yes." It is finally safe to deal with economic empowerment without offending the establishment.

During our "struggle" to gain high political office and a little influence on the powerbrokers, our high-level corporate jobs that pay millions, and the notion that we had "made it," we felt it was not safe to discuss economic empowerment. After all, why rock the boat and talk about Black people getting our true collective freedom, especially since some of us had already gained our individual freedom? It was not safe then because we could lose our individual creature comforts and newly found status.

So for the last thirty-five years we acquiesced to the ridiculous notion that we had made tremendous progress. Now we find ourselves, having followed the leaders who chose individualism over collectivism and politics over economics, mired in last place in the wealth-building race.

But Economic Empowerment is in vogue now. The Jacksons (father and son) are saying this is our next great fight—the fourth movement of a freedom symphony—with the release of their new book, "It's About The Money." While I am glad he and others are getting the word out, I hope and trust their brand of economic empowerment is collective rather than individual. I hope they incorporate the theme that is also in vogue now: "Leave no one behind."

The other issue that amazes me is that now, after three decades, Brother Jackson has come to the conclusion that it's all about the money. It's always been about the money—even in 1968. Why does it take us so long to wake up? Or, is it that we have been awake all the time, only with a different (individual) agenda?

The Jacksons are using analogies, metaphors, and other flowery language to describe our current economic condition and what we should do about it. They describe the first movement of our symphony as Black people getting our freedom from slavery. The second movement is centered on Black people fighting and overcoming segregation. The third revolves around Black people securing the right to vote. And the fourth and current movement is wealth-building (economic empowerment) - for everyone.

The consistent term (or note) in the first three movements is "Black People." That term is obviously missing in the final movement. It is strange, now that Black people have achieved the first three movements, the fourth movement is centered on everyone, i.e., minorities and women. This sounds like those Black Rights (13th, 14th, and 15th Amendments) that soon turned to "Civil Rights," and became a stick that others used to beat Black people down.

Will somebody please help me understand what makes any of our leaders think we are obligated to help everyone else achieve their wealth? Haven't we already created wealth for everyone else as slave laborers, as consumers, and as corporate executives? What would make us think we are able to help everyone else as we make feeble attempts to help ourselves? Here we are on the bottom of the economic heap, and the Jacksons are suggesting that we, of all people, are going to form a movement that will empower all "minorities" and women. The only people talking about "diversity" are Black people, as if we have the obligation and the power to change someone's mind about Black people.

As I once wrote about this kind of thinking, before an airplane takes off someone gives instructions about the oxygen masks. They say if there is an emergency put your mask on first, and then help someone else. The same principle applies to our economic situation as Black people. We must help our own people and stop this delusion we have about "rainbows" and "minorities" and other politically correct titles. Most "minorities" are miles ahead of us anyway. What do we look like saying we are going to help them? We can hardly help ourselves.

Is it safe? Is it safe? Is it safe? Well, Black people, being 135 years removed from slavery, having given our lives for this country, having enriched all sectors and groups with our dollars, and having the most education of any Black people in the world today, I would say it is definitely safe.

It's safe to support your brothers' and sisters' business. It's safe to invest in your community. It's safe to love and trust one another. It's safe to be seen with another Black person. It's safe to work for the economic empowerment of Black people. It's safe not to mention "minorities and women." Yes, it is safe to **BE BLACK!**

I hope and trust that we as Black people will finally stop doing what we have done since 1965. If we do not, we will continue to get the same results we have always gotten. And, leaders, please stop deluding our people with the notion that we can achieve Black economic empowerment by creating economic empowerment for everyone else. They already have theirs; let's go get ours. It's always been about the money—**Our Money.**

Politics – The Rules of the Game

There are reports to the effect that in some sections the black man has difficulty in voting and having counted the little white ballot which he has the privilege of depositing about twice every two years. But there is a little green ballot that he can vote through the teller's window 313 days in every year and no one will throw it out or refuse to count it. The man that has the property, the intelligence, the character, is the one that is going to have the largest share in controlling the government, whether he is white or black, or whether in the North or South. It is important that all of the privileges of the law be ours; but it is more important that we be prepared for the exercise of these privileges. Booker T. Washington, *Indianapolis Sentinel,* April 23, 1896.

Another election is upon us and, at least in my neck of the woods, much of what I hear is the same tired rhetoric about the importance of simply casting a vote. This time, so they say, we must show up at the polls in great numbers; this time we must make sure as many Black people as possible cast their votes; this time, we can change the political landscape of this country—if we only "get out the vote"—this time, as we have been told so many times before.

Well, once again it seems Brother Booker T. was correct. When will we heed his lessons? He and others warned us not to place all of our eggs in the political basket, but there are some that would have us believe our salvation lies in politics alone. We elected some 8,000 public officials during the 30-year period from 1960 through 1990, several of whom were mayors of the largest cities in this country. How much economic progress did we make during that same 30-year period? Sure, we needed to be involved in the political system, but we also needed to make significant strides in the economic system. In other words, while we were busy garnering our "civil rights" we should have also been actively engaged in obtaining our "silver rights."

This is not a criticism of those who fought so hard during those years and those who held those public offices, although some did absolutely nothing to further the collective economic status of Black people. Rather, this is a clarion call for us to finally stop putting most of our emphasis on politics and so little of our energy on economic empowerment.

One thing is for sure—Economics runs politics. As much as we would like to believe the contrary, Black people will not gain the kinds of political benefits that accrue to other groups until we learn how to play the political game. We will never move beyond the *pomp and circumstance* phase of politics until we put our money where our mouths are. That is, contribute to the campaigns of Black candidates as well as others that act in our best interests. No contributions—no accountability—no *quid pro quo*. That's the rule of the game.

The other reality is that if we do not create our own economic base, via ownership of land, development of vertically integrated businesses, and the establishment of business organizations, such as Black Chambers of Commerce, we will still be an afterthought when it comes to political concessions and benefits. I cannot think of any group in this country that has made significant political progress without first building an economic infrastructure from which to leverage political favors. Can you?

Marcus Garvey said, *The most important area for the exercise of independent effort (is) economic. After a people have established successfully a firm foundation they naturally turn to politics and society, but not first to society and politics, because the two latter cannot exist without the former.*

T. Thomas Fortune said, *No people ever became great and prosperous by devoting their infant energies to politics. We were literally born into political responsibility before we had mastered the economic conditions which underlie these duties.*

How many more lessons and warnings do we need? Sure, another election is upon us, but we cannot continue to think that by simply casting our individual votes everything will be all right. We cannot continue to vote and then retreat to our homes, back to business as usual—maintaining the economic status quo. If we are going to play in the political game we must play by the rules, and MONEY rules the political game. If you are not willing to put some of your money on the table, you may as well fold your hand.

Politics alone will continue to keep Black people where we are now—at the bottom of the economic heap, depending upon someone to throw a few crumbs our way. We will continue to be at the mercy of those who have well-established economic systems which allow their dollars to circulate among themselves several times prior to leaving their communities.

Do you want to see another two years, four years, or six years go by, during which time Black people wring our hands about what the politicians are not doing for us? Do you want to see us continuously whining about the political inequities that abound in our neighborhoods? Do you want to see our children grow up with the same political pipe dreams in which many of us were taught to believe?

If your answers are "NO," while you are in that voting booth (and that is certainly where you should be) think also about what you will do to build and sustain our economic interests. Think about the comments of Booker T. and Marcus Garvey and Thomas Fortune. Learn about the many other brothers and sisters who promoted economic strategies for Black people and tried with every fiber in their bodies to make us understand the importance of self-help, ownership, and control of resources. Learn the rules of the game, before it's too late. If we build a strong economic system for Black people, we will no longer have to worry about our politics.

The Black List

The May 2000 edition of "Ebony Magazine" features a new list of the most influential Blacks. I am always interested in seeing this list because I am intrigued by the notion of *influence versus power*. I like to see which Black people are being portrayed as the "movers and shakers" of our time. And I always look through the list to find the people who are most influential—and leading the way—when it comes to economic empowerment.

Two things struck me as I looked through the list. One thing was the absence of certain people; the other was the very first person featured in the story. I will start with the latter. The newly appointed Chairman and CEO of Avis Rent A Car, Mr. Barry Rand, a perennial high ranking Black in corporate America for years, heads the list of "100+ Influential Black Americans."

So what's the problem, you say? Well, most of us know what happened to Avis last year. It joined a long list of companies that got caught with their discrimination showing and had complaints filed against it for disparate practices against Black patrons. You have heard it so many times before with Revlon, Coca Cola, Texaco, Denny's, Comp USA, et al, so I will not repeat the story.

The problem is this. The companies in question, and we know who they are, always seem to successfully recapture the business of Black consumers by hiring a Black person, doing commercials and other advertising campaigns featuring Black people, and giving Black consumers "deals" to return to their stores by offering apologies and discounts.

Avis was caught. Shortly thereafter, we see Mr. Rand's picture in **USA Today** as the *new man in charge*. We also begin to see, as I did recently, television commercials featuring Black counter clerks and Black *satisfied customers* doing business with Avis. This same scenario has happened so many times it's almost comical, and it would be if it were not so sad.

Please do not misunderstand this message. I am proud of Mr. Rand and his accomplishments. I hope he will turn his new company around and use his "influence" in a way that will "trickle down" to the masses of Black people. I hope and trust he will be a leader who will use his influence to educate Black people, to economically empower Black people, to publicly speak out for Black people, and to assist Black people in our quest for psychological and economic freedom. And this is not a request solely for Mr. Rand; I hope all of the "100+ Most Influential Black Americans" will do the same.

The article's lack of Black men and women who are promoting economic empowerment—full time, for the masses—was also quite striking. Again, nothing against those who are featured, many of who have done quite well with their personal economic empowerment. They are well deserving of the recognition they received. But, don't you think that on any list of most influential Blacks we should see a few Black people who are leading the charge for *collective* economic empowerment?

Why do we not see Dr. Claud Anderson, author of **Black Labor White Wealth**, nationally influential leader and educator? Dr. Anderson has hundreds of thousands of followers and subscribers to his economic empowerment strategies. His principles of **Powernomics** and his educational forums have influenced millions of Black people across this country. Why do we not see him on the list? Or on television shows like Oprah and Tavis?

Where are Al Wellington and Ken Bridges? These two gentlemen have influenced thousands of Black brothers and sisters from coast to coast with their establishment of the **MATAH Network**. They have demonstrated leadership in the fight for collective economic freedom. Have you seen them on any list?

Others obviously missing from the list of Most Influential Black people were George Fraser, Brooke Stephens, Tony Brown, Julianne Malveaux, and Magic Johnson. These and others are dedicated to empowering our people economically, which is second only in importance to our spiritual empowerment. We need a list for them too. Our people need to know who these people are and what they are doing. Our people need to know there are men and women working everyday on their behalf vis-a-vis our collective economic future—our children's future.

Why do we seem so disinclined to promote our brothers and sisters who are leading the charge for economic empowerment for the masses of Black people? I beg those who are "Most Influential" in Black media to please uplift our brothers and sisters who are fighting for economic freedom. They are indeed influential, but they must, no **WE** must be able to transform that influence into power.

There is a huge difference between mere economic influence and real economic power. If Black people settle for influence only, we will remain in our current economic condition. We must understand the words of Amos Wilson who wrote, *The idea that the Afrikan American community can exercise effective power, political, or otherwise, without simultaneously exercising economic power, is a fantasy. Hundreds... may attain positions of influence and affluence... [but] millions of average Afrikan Americans are marginalized and impoverished simultaneously.*

Use your influence to secure collective economic power for our people, please.

If We Are So Smart, Why Are We So Far Behind?

I am quite concerned about the fact that, according to George Fraser, Black people have accumulated some $5 trillion in intellectual capital since 1968. I am concerned that we as Black people have achieved tremendous individual acclaim at the most prestigious institutions in the land. I am perplexed by Black intellectuals who remain in their ivory towers, behind their ivy-draped walls, and simply speak or write on the subject of economic empowerment.

It seems to me that with all of our intelligence, all of our knowledge, we should be much further along in this country when it comes to our collective economic status. Why aren't we? Surely we can figure our way out of our current economic situation. After all, our forefathers and mothers figured it out; and many of them had very little formal education. What's our problem?

Is it that we still have not adopted a national or even a local strategy for the economic uplift of our people? Several have been offered. T.M. Pryor, author of **Wealthbuilding Lessons of Booker T. Washington**, offers a plan that entails pooling our resources. Dr. Claud Anderson, author of **Black Labor, White Wealth**, offers a strategy for vertically integrated business development. Tony Brown, author of **Black Lies, White Lies**, promotes an economic strategy centered on technology.

And we have several others who are advocating financial and entrepreneurial strategies for Black economic empowerment. What more do we need? Why won't we adopt one or more of these positions and move forward? Could it be that some of us are more concerned about our individual status than our collective economic status? Are some of us allowing our egos to supercede our common sense?

We have Black professors of economics, financial experts, and tremendously successful businesspersons who could, if they were so inclined, lead our people out of the doldrums of economic despair. So why are we still locked-in to second-class status and moving swiftly to third-class?

My contention is that we are constrained by psychological barriers, placed among us by white people with third-grade educations, that we are simply unable to tear down. Despite all of our capability, all of our intellect, and all of our economic resources, we languish at the bottom of the economic heap in this country. Folks, that has to be psychological, because it is so illogical. It makes absolutely no sense, especially when we have been shown the way by so many of our brothers and sisters.

According to a recent PBS documentary narrated by Henry Louis Gates, W.E.B. DuBois was disenchanted by his so-called Talented Tenth because they saw their achieved economic, intellectual, and political status as the end rather than the means. In other words they failed to reach back to those less fortunate and take care of our race, as DuBois had envisioned.

Harold Cruse, noted author, suggests that Black people who have represented the Talented Tenth in the civil rights and intellectual leadership have led the Black masses not toward self-reliance and economic freedom but toward dependency and expropriation.

Again, I ask the question: If we are so smart, why are we so far behind? I think we have fallen prey to the elitism that runs rampant through our communities. I think we have succumbed to the brainwashing of those who would have us remain dependent. And I think we suffer from a psychological malady that, if not cured, will keep Black people at the bottom of the economic heap for years to come. Oh sure, individuals among us will continue to hold themselves up and be held up by others as paragons of success. But what will that matter if we as a collective body of people continue to digress—or even maintain status quo?

We are too smart to allow this situation to continue. Does it make a lot of sense for poor Black people to continue to parade after their affluent leaders seeking more political positions, more jobs in major corporations, and more sensitivity classes? Those are not the outcomes we should seek for economic empowerment.

So here's another question: If our actions of the past forty years have not achieved economic empowerment, why are we still following them?

Section Five

Money, Money, Money

Is [capitalism] bad or is it the men who control the system? I do not believe capitalism is bad any more than I believe money is evil. Furthermore, I don't believe that African Americans should be ashamed to call themselves capitalists.
Kelvin Boston

When you can count your money, you ain't got none.
Don King

The O'Jays sure had it right, didn't they? Some people will do just about anything for that "mean green." The next series of writings deals with the positive and negative aspects of money—Black money. We talk a lot about creating wealth, but we do not stop to think about the fact that while we do create a great deal of wealth, that wealth is for someone else. We must learn to retain the wealth we create.

Money, like it or not, rules this country. Black people have a lot of it. Black people spend a lot of it. Money can be a blessing or it can be a curse. It is up to us what impact money—our money - will have on our future. If we manage it correctly, cooperatively, and collectively we can achieve all the things we discuss in our "economic summits."

Managing our money appropriately can get persons who work in our best interests elected to public office. By using our money wisely we can have the kinds of businesses we need to build a legacy for our children. There are so many things we can do if we would just take care of our money.

The downside is that some of us will make *Faustian* deals for little or nothing, deals that result in the demise of another brother or sister. That's the shame of money and what it does to some of us.

Now let me get this straight. Black people have enough money that if we were a separate country we'd rank maybe 10th in the world, right? We have several multi-millionaire entertainers and athletes, right? We donate approximately $20 billion a year to our churches, right?

Now, the flip-side is that we spend 95% of our money on goods and services made and offered by people who are not Black, right? Nationally, we own only 20 supermarkets, right? We have very few Black-owned banks, right? We own fewer than 20 hotels in the entire country, right? We do not even control the distribution of our own hair care products, right?

You do the math and I am sure you will agree, there is something drastically wrong with the Black economy in the United States. What are YOU willing to do about it?

We have crusaders like Brooke Stephens, Julieanne Malveaux, Charles Ross, Kelvin Boston, and many others telling us how to use our money wisely. We have the economic lessons taught us by A.G. Gaston, Martin Delaney, S.B. Fuller, Madame C.J. Walker and hundreds of other Black brothers and sisters.

Moreover, we have more than enough money to do something great for our people and to leave a proud and prosperous legacy for our children. Will we allow our money to be a blessing, or will we allow it to be a curse?

The answer lies within us all. I hope we do the right thing.

$533 Billion in Black Buying "Weakness"

As we brag about all the money we earn each year we must also take into account how much we spend. Some have called it Black buying *power,* myself included. But I think it would be more appropriately characterized as Black buying *weakness.* Why? Because we spend far too many of our hard-earned dollars with businesses other than our own.

Our weakness for spending our money so frivolously and without reciprocity in the marketplace is exemplified by the glaring statistic publicized by the Selig Center in Atlanta. The Center's research indicates that Black people will have generated $533 billion by the end of 1999. The other very vital statistic is that we, Black people, spend approximately 7% of that $533 billion with Black owned businesses.

To further amplify our economic position we need only to look at how many individuals and corporations have been made tremendously wealthy through the purchasing habits of Black consumers. Clothing manufacturers especially have made boatloads of money from Black people as well as those "middlemen" in the Black hair care industry. Thus, I will refer to our buying "power" as buying "weakness."

In light of our buying weakness, it is reasonable to suggest that we must practice economic principles that redirect and slow down Black spending. To do that, we must not be afraid or reluctant to make economic sacrifices for our own people. We must encourage Black consumers to THINK about our expenditures, to ask the questions: Who is getting my money? What are they doing with it? Are my people receiving any benefit from it? Do those with whom I do business respect me?

Of course we must hold our own businesses accountable as well, and they must meet a standard that does not allow them to sell mediocre goods and services to us. Just as we have choices among general market businesses, we also have choices among Black owned businesses, and we should exercise those choices. The billions we spend each year will continue to be disrespected and taken for granted if we do not exercise informed choices in our purchasing habits.

So why are we so weak when it comes to spending our money? Well, historically we have been programmed to believe that if we possess certain items we have "made it." We have been taught to believe that owning something with someone's name or even someone's number on it is valuable and will increase our self-esteem. We have even been programmed to believe the ridiculous notion that the more we pay for an item the more status we receive. As Sharazad Ali says, *Black people brag about how **much** we pay for things, and white people brag about how **little** they pay.* The sad thing about that statement is that it is absolutely true—whether we want to admit it or not.

That's why we should start calling our $533 billion "buying" weakness rather than "buying" power. Power suggests the ability to effect change, either positively or negatively. Well, we have caused a great change in the wealth of others (positive), but we have not increased the wealth of our own people with our own money (negative). So how can we continue to refer to our purchasing habits as "power"? Of course, others can and should refer to it as "power" because of what it has done for them. But when it comes to what our money has done for us, we must refer to it as "weakness."

How do we change this scenario? We must rechannel our spending away from everyone else and more toward ourselves. Buy Black-manufactured, Black-distributed, and Black-retailed products. Use Black service providers to meet your needs. Refer potential business to Black entrepreneurs. Form alliances and partnerships among Black businesses to go after larger pieces of business. Spend our dollars with Black-owned media. Be willing to give up a little "convenience" to support a Black business.

I think most if not all Black people realize our economic situation is in a state of emergency. One of the big problems is that too few of us are willing to make the changes necessary to maintain the wealth that we create each year. Some of us are walking, and too many of us are just talking. Some of us are serving, and many of us are swerving (ducking and dodging—trying to stay out of the line of fire). Some of us are leading, and many of us are pleading (begging for someone else to come to our rescue). Some of us have focus, and some of us are bogus. Some of us are working, and some of us are lurking (in the shadows – afraid to come out and be seen).

Please make a commitment to do your part to change our economic situation in this country. Please commit to less creation of wealth for others and more for Black people. Resolve to do what you can to move us to the economic position we deserve and must have in order for our children and grandchildren to survive in this country. Instill in yourself and in those with whom you come in contact the principle of reciprocity in the marketplace. Incorporate "critical thinking" in your life and use it to fashion a personal plan of action for the economic uplift of yourself, your family, and your people.

Until we change our purchasing habits, we will always have tremendous ***buying weakness*** rather than ***buying power***.

BLACKONOMIC$

Collective and Cooperative Economics—
Middle East Style

In my book, **Economic Empowerment or Economic Enslavement—We have a choice**, there is a discussion regarding "manufactured oil prices" and some of the other games being run on us much of the time. It draws the reader's attention to how easy it is for those in control of various facets of our economy to increase their profits and to make their lives even more comfortable—anytime they want.

We see it now with the rising fuel costs. People in cold climates must choose between warming their homes and putting food on the table. Over-the-road truckers are faced with sky-rocketing diesel fuel costs. Automobile owners cringe each time they pull up to the pump. Where it used to be a fill-up, it's now maybe a half tank or so.

What we are facing with these rising costs is another example of people working together to improve their financial position. They are working cooperatively to strengthen their collective economic position. Whether they need the extra billions or not is irrelevant; they are in control of their resources and they determine what others will pay for those resources.

A few little countries in the Middle East got together and realized they could control much of the world by simply working in concert. A few little countries, several of which the United States has sent men and women to fight and die for, get together and decide how much oil they are going to produce and, thereby, change the landscape of many larger countries of the world. Well, that's what collective economics is all about.

This dazzling display of cooperative economics is something each of us can witness personally at least once each week when we pull up to the pump. We should learn from it. A few small countries working together brought big bad truckers to their knees, caused them to drive to our nation's capital in protest, and set up "rolling road blocks"

106

along our expressways in the summer of 2000. A few small potentates made the rest of us rant and rave about the price of gasoline, shake and shiver in our own homes, and cut back on other essentials.

This example of collective and cooperative economics, while it is not one that benefits us, does benefit those who participate in it, and Black people should use this example to develop our own cooperative economic structure. We should assess our resources, both intellectual and financial, and establish programs and procedures that will benefit our people. It's a matter of controlling what we have and doling it out at our discretion, not at the request of someone else.

You can see it with the OPEC states. They do not seem to care that some of our people died for their countries, that some of them came back home with illnesses that will eventually kill them, or that our people saved their precious oil by putting out those oil-well fires. That does not matter when it comes to the money. They understand that what they have is power and they can exercise that power anytime they wish to do so.

An analogy can be drawn between what OPEC is doing and what Black people could be doing in this country. If we were psychologically free and really decided to pursue our true economic freedom, we could bring a few folks to their knees as well. We could transform what is now an insignificant group of consumers into a powerful band of producers, distributors, and retailers.

We could wreak havoc on the corporations that take our dollars for granted. We could cause an economic tidal wave rather than the small ripples we currently see as a result of our half-hearted boycotts, demands for apologies, organizational payoffs, token employees, and all of the other shallow tactics we deploy and accept.

Black people could be the OPEC of this country if we would use our half-trillion dollars to build our own businesses and to determine the prices of our products rather than having always to submit to the price-gouging of other businesses. If we took control of our resources and worked cooperatively and collectively, in support of one another, withdrawing our dollars from those who hold us in disdain, we could control our economic destiny.

If we would deny our dollars, not for one day, but for one year or more, to those businesses that exploit our people on a daily basis and return virtually nothing, we could be in control. Have you ever wondered what happened to National Gas Out Day? The trouble with that campaign was that it lasted for just one day. On May 20, 2000, we had National Black Out Day. Did we accomplish anything, especially if we simply returned to our normal buying habits the very next day?

Take a lesson from the little countries about whom we sometimes joke and make fun. They are demonstrating the purest form of collective and cooperative economics. They are making us pay dearly because they are in control of their resources. Black people should do the same.

It's About the Money

As one peels back the layers of an onion the odor gets increasingly stronger. The closer one gets to the core of the onion the more difficult it is for one not to cry. The same principle holds true in most circles of our society, except it's not onions we are peeling, it's the seedy sides of political, social, educational and, sad to say, some religious organizations. It always—sooner or later—boils down to the M-O-N-E-Y.

Take Paula Jones (please). At first it was about getting her "good name" back. I always wondered how she lost her good name in the first place, especially if she did not do what she claimed the President asked her to do. She said she did not want money, and if she received any she would donate it to charity. Yeah, right. When the real deal came to light, "Miss Paula," as Ken Hamblin would call her, asked for a tidy little sum of $1,000,000.00. It wasn't for attorneys' fees; they were paid for by outside parties. What's up, Paula? Was it really just about the money?

While we're on politics. Do you really believe that votes are what most of our politicos are looking for? Do you think for one second that most of them do not first decide how much money they will need to get elected rather than how many votes? Do you think that most politicians fight for those who vote for them and put their contributors on the back burner? If you do, I have some oceanfront property in Kansas I'd like to sell to you.

Money drives the political system and most other systems in this country. When *renaissance* Black people finally get that through our hard heads we will do much better economically. Our forefathers and mothers knew that. What's the problem with us, the most educated Black people on the face of the earth?

Many of us seem to think that getting mad, changing our votes ("And if he doesn't do right we'll vote him out in four years") demonstrating, having sensitivity training, or getting a windfall from a lawsuit will somehow change our collective economic status. News flash! They will not. Sure those are tools at our disposal, but if they are all we rely upon we are in deep trouble. Look at our economic condition now after forty years of trying the same tactics to uplift our people. According to the data, collectively, we have failed miserably.

While we are busy marching outside someone's store or business, we should also be pooling our resources and buying our own supermarket, hotel, restaurant, newspaper, or any other business we would like to have. We just seem to find it so difficult to let Pharaoh go. We continue to want to be near him; we want to support his businesses whether he wants our business or not—and then we complain that he treats us unkindly.

While we are busy complaining about those "Arabs" and those "Koreans" and those "Indians" selling us bad products and over-charging us, we could be establishing our own businesses in our own neighborhoods and stop shopping at the businesses about which we complain. I guess it just feels good to whine about something rather than do the work necessary to change our situation. Do you think that were it not for the profits these "outsider" businesses make, they would even be in Black neighborhoods? Do you think those Koreans who stood in front of their stores with guns during the L.A. (Rodney King) riots would be in South Central or Watts everyday, risking life and limb, if they were not making tons of money?

Yes, it's all about the money; it's nearly always about the money. This country has $100 million Empowerment Zones, billions going into Welfare-to-Work programs, more billions being spent for new public housing by HUD, and still more being dumped into Travel and Tourism. Who is getting that money? While many of us are arguing about insignificant issues, trying to prove how much we know about the laws and regulations, pontificating on procedure and "Robots' Rules of Order," big businesses are positioning themselves to get the lion's share of these public funds. Black people are relegated to the role of *pass-through* for billions of dollars, and if we wake up one morning and find we have been hood-winked, again, we will pull out our marching shoes and our megaphones. Business owners will cast a disparaging eye our way on their way to the bank. It's about the money.

I don't know about you, but I am tired of us attempting to use leverage that we do not have. We simply are not players in the economic arena of this country. Bill Gates' assets alone equal more than 10% of the entire annual income of Black people. It makes no sense at all for us to continue fooling ourselves, pretending that we are capable of helping every other group in the U.S. If we fail to create vertically integrated businesses, jobs for our people, and other institutions, we will have failed in the stewardship of our own economic stability.

According to **Urban Call**, a monthly periodical published by **Segmented Market Services, Inc.** In Winston-Salem, North Carolina, Black people own nineteen (19) supermarkets in the entire country. Folks, we cannot even sell ourselves the very basic sustenance required to live because we have yet to figure out that it's all about the money. We spend a lot of it, the majority of which is with businesses other than our own. Those business owners live off two incomes—100% of theirs and 95% of ours. That's shameful.

Economic empowerment must be elevated to the top of our agenda—not just rhetorically—it must be action-oriented. We must do what everyone else is doing in this country if we are going to survive collectively. We must make our presence felt with our dollars, and that means withdrawing those dollars from others and using them for our own benefit first.

There is nothing wrong with self-interest, especially when it comes to the money, because when it's all said and done—**It's all about the money**. Right, Paula?

Black Out Day

There was a call to action on the Internet for Black people to participate in a National Black Out Day. On May 20, 2000, Blacks were asked to refrain from spending <u>any money</u>. If we absolutely had to spend, we were asked to spend with Black owned businesses. The reason being given for the Black Out was to show corporations and other businesses in this country how much money Black people spend as well as to demonstrate our economic impact.

While I supported the effort, I also offered some additional direction on this matter. First of all, to refuse to spend for just one day and then go back to doing business as usual the very next day does nothing to improve the economic status of Black people. As for showing the establishment how much we spend and how great a role we play in their economy, they already know how much we spend, what we spend it on, and virtually every other aspect of our buying habits. Check out Ken Smikle's **Target Market News**, or just go to your local library and do some research on consumption spending by Black people.

Our buying habits, as well as our economic impact on business, are well documented. Believe me—they already know.

So what will "showing them" do for US? I submit, very little or absolutely nothing. I am for withdrawing our money as much as possible from as many non-Black owned businesses as possible, but I am also for doing something that will have a positive impact on Black businesses and Black consumers. If we concentrate merely on hurting someone else or proving a point for a day, such as Gas Out Day in 1999 (Look at gas prices now and you can see how much impact we had on that industry) we will not achieve the goal of our protest: economic empowerment.

We must incorporate positive action in our strategies of protest and boycotts so that our people benefit from our actions. How many Black people are now buying Texaco gas? How many of us are eating at Denny's? How many of us are renting cars from Avis? How many Blacks are collecting bottle caps for Coca Cola? How many of you have turned in your 10% discount coupons at Comp USA?

Another example is the controversial state flag issue in South Carolina. Did Black people gain economically when the flag was taken down? It was back to business as usual with Black people getting little or nothing from the tourism industry in South Carolina. That kind of strategy makes no economic sense. Or maybe it does, to those Black people who get paid off to say "Everything is fine now, you can come back to South Carolina and spend your money, Black people."

The result of our being angry and protesting should be economic empowerment, collective economic empowerment, not a few individuals getting paid, a few nice commercials on television, or a new "hired hand" with a Black face for showcasing purposes only. The result of our being mad at someone should result in our making positive moves toward getting true freedom, both psychological and economic.

Demonstrations of our anger alone will not do that. Only positive action toward one another will get us there. Going back to the status quo after the fight is over does nothing for Black people economically. Protests of this kind must go on for much longer than one day, and they must not merely concentrate on causing a little uneasiness for someone else. We cannot and must not allow our anger to be the only driving force. It's not about "them," it's about us.

Please think about this and know that we must not only make a point by withholding our money on one day, we must also look at ways to enrich ourselves as a result of our actions. Those stores we didn't shop at on May 20th are still there and probably making just as much or more after we "proved our point."

Now, what is the answer? What shall we do? Well, here is one answer. How about a Black Dollar Day? Let's call for Black people on May 20th to take one of those dollars they do not spend and start a Black fund in their city. Thereafter, on the 20th of every month, let's continue to do that. One dollar, each month, from every Black person who cares to participate, deposited in a Black financial institution, if possible. Now that's what I call proving a point. That's what I call demonstrating Black economic impact. Just think what can be done across this nation in our various cities if we would do that. Withholding our dollars from someone else and using those same dollars to empower ourselves - to support ourselves. What a concept!

I don't know how large your city is, so I will use mine as an example. Cincinnati has over 100,000 Black citizens. If just half of us participated in Black Dollar Day, we could invest in new businesses and community projects, build and support our own institutions, and help those among us who are less fortunate or those who run into difficulties from time to time. Who knows? You may be the next one to need help. Isn't a $1.00 per month investment worth it?

Get your Black Dollar Day started now. I have already called for one in our city. How about you?

Blacks Folks on Tour

Have you ever given any thought to how much African Americans participate in the Travel and Tourism industry? Ever wondered, just a little, how much money we spend traveling and attending events? There are the "biggies" like Music and Art Festivals, Expos, and football games. Then there are the hundreds of religious conferences, social functions, and just plain parties we attend all over this country and now in other countries.

Black people spend billions on travel and tourism, most of which goes to businesses other than our own. Before you start giving me the excuses for our expenditures, you know, "We don't own any hotels," or "We don't own convention centers," or "We don't control the concessions," let's look at ways we can benefit from our zest for meetings, conventions, festivals, and tourism.

First of all we must understand the industry and be aware of the role we play in it. When Black people travel we stay longer, spend more money, and take more persons with us than most other groups. That alone should be enough for us to at least get the respect and reciprocity we deserve from those who benefit from our dollars, "but nooo," they will continue to take our tourism dollars and return as few as possible to us in sponsorships, advertising, and the like. Sure they will. Wouldn't you?

That's where we come in; that's where you come in. Since it's obvious that we are unwilling to follow Tony Brown's advice of ten or fifteen years ago (seems we keep repeating the same mistakes) and stop convening our meetings for one year, here are some other things we can do.

First, we can form businesses and organizations that can take advantage of the tremendous opportunities in travel and tourism. Via our Black Chamber of Commerce here in Cincinnati, we developed our own tourism division. Our general goal is to solicit conventions, tourists, and family reunions to our city and, more importantly, when they come, to assure our Black-owned businesses are in a position to benefit from the ensuing economic impact.

Maybe we do not own any hotels or convention centers, but we do have caterers, florists, security firms, tour companies, T-shirt vendors, photographers, computer technicians, audio/visual experts, meeting planners, book stores, restaurants, beauty and barber shops, boutiques, and art galleries. I could go on, but I am sure you get the picture.

But bringing people to town is one thing, being prepared to do business when they come is another. We work with our member businesses to assure they can deliver what we promise. Business capacity is most important—Black business capacity. We can complain all we want about other businesses getting all of the action, but if we are not prepared and if we cannot deliver the goods, people will seek other outlets for goods and services. If we are prepared and if we are good, we will get the business—not because we are Black, but because we are good.

Get involved with travel and tourism in your city and make it a major part of your economic empowering strategy. We are talking about a multi-billion dollar industry to which Black people contribute more than our proportionate share. Shouldn't we be getting something from it? We travel all over the country and stay in the finest hotels, eat and drink only the best, and spend, spend, spend while we are there.

Someone throws a party and we come in droves. After the party we go home and talk about what a good time we had. They go to the bank. Let's start throwing some parties of our own. Then we will really have something to celebrate.

Music festivals, football games, and other predominantly Black events will generate billions during the balance of this year. Will the Black owned businesses in your city benefit from them? To what degree will they benefit? Will these events create opportunities for new Black owned businesses? These are the questions we must ask and act upon.

Kenneth Price, of Triad Development, LLC in Cincinnati, Ohio, completed an analysis of the Travel and Tourism industry. In his report he cites, *Black people participate heavily on the demand side of the tourism industry. We must develop business strategies and form consortia that will position Black people on the supply side of this multi-billion dollar industry.*

I contend that we miss out on opportunities that are before us everyday, many times because we get diverted by emotional causes and impractical strategies that do not lead to true economic empowerment. I also contend that tourism is a great place to start for true freedom for Black people. If we are going to continue to come to someone else's parties, let's make sure we take home some real party favors.

Substituting Holidays for Holy Days

This year, as in years gone by, we will see Black people run to the malls and department stores to spend a large part of our half trillion dollars on gifts and other items in the name of Christmas. Prior to that, we will witness our people rushing to those same outlets on the day after Thanksgiving to do the same thing. And then, next year during Easter, we will once again spend millions on clothing, eggs, and chocolate. All of this will be done in the name of holidays.

While everyone seems to get into the act of buying during the holidays, my concern is of course centered on the purchasing habits of Black people. Why? Because we are the primary targets of the marketing campaigns and spend more of our disposable income during these "holidays" than other consumer groups in this country. In addition, I am concerned because we can least afford to keep spending our money the way we do.

More importantly, Black people, as religious as we claim to be, have allowed our *Holy Days* to be turned into *Holidays* by greedy retailers. We sit back each year and allow them to ratchet-up their sales campaigns, extend their hours of operation, and even play on our sympathy when they do not meet their sales forecasts during Christmas. And, boy, do we more than make up for it during those after-Christmas sales.

I wonder what would happen if the merchants would do the same kinds of sales campaigns during Ramadan or Hanukkah. Do you think they would get away with it? I don't. Outrage by Islamic and Jewish groups would be the order of the day. The merchants would undoubtedly be severely punished by these groups as they withhold their dollars from the offending stores thereafter.

This is not solely a Black issue; it is a Christian issue. I am just amazed at the acquiescence of Christians, Black and white, who participate and make these "holidays" the most profitable of the year. We let others turn our Holy

Days into their holidays for the sole purpose of making billions of dollars—for themselves.

Don't you think it's time we stop this madness? The religious implications are bad enough, but Black people especially should have had enough of this kind of exploitation by now. Who turned these Holy Days into holidays anyway? Did Black people do this? I remember when I was growing up in the 1950's, every Easter I would get a new suit—the only suit my parents could afford to buy each year. On Christmas we would get whatever toys they could afford as well. I don't remember any special shopping that took place after Thanksgiving, but this kind of "holiday" buying has been going on for a long time.

So where did it come from? Bingo! The retailers. We, the consumers, have been lulled into a state of shopping euphoria during our Holy Days, and we have essentially abandoned the real meaning and tradition behind them. We have allowed the *moneychangers* to return to the temple, and we should be ashamed of ourselves.

Moreover, Black consumers, those who can least afford to participate in these no-win holiday shopping sprees, are the first in line and the ones who spend the most on the most ridiculous items. It is a time for us to move further into debt, a time to max-out those credit cards, and a time to create even more wealth for businesses other than our own. What a deal!

Black consumers have a penchant for loading up on items that will be obsolete in a few months, and although I understand the history behind our reasons for doing this, it is definitely time to put it to an end. And what better time to do this than during the next "holiday" season?

As Black people look for ways to make an impact, to gain economic reciprocity, to increase our leverage, and to *level the playing field,* the answers are right in front of us. All we have to do is refrain from our conspicuous consumption during the holiday season. If we must spend money during that time, why not set up our own bazaars in

119

which Black vendors and other Black business owners can sell their wares and services? That way we would be killing two birds with one stone: Bringing back the respect we have lost for our Holy Days; and redirecting a portion of our tremendous spending toward one another.

We would begin to take charge and let the retailers and corporations know that we are no longer willing to be their profit margins; we are no longer going to keep them "in the Black"; and we will continue to work together for our own economic uplift.

Now that's the very kind of action that would warrant a brand new holiday. It would surely be worth celebrating the day that Black people finally decided to make a drastic change in our economic destiny. What better time than this Christmas? We could end the year on a high note and begin the next year on an even higher note by rallying our consumers and by using our dollars as the economic weapons they are. Talk about Ujamaa—it would be a fantastic celebration!

Let's face it. The only way for Black people to make a real move toward economic power in this country is to withhold our dollars from others and direct them toward our own economic efforts, such as business development and business support. We cannot afford to continue being the victims of economic exploitation; we cannot allow our children's future to be mortgaged; and we must not get mired in credit card debt, especially if we want to move beyond our current status as the biggest and most generous consumer segment in the world.

In Cincinnati (or Cincinn-apathy, as I call it) where I live, our group, the Black United Front, called for economic sanctions against the downtown businesses. We have a Black owned shopping center and we are asking our people to shop there. We are also seeking vendors and other businesses to bring their sales items to the mall and sell them there. I would love to see Black people give 100% support to this effort, like the brothers and sisters did in South Africa prior to the fall of *apartheid*, but I kind of doubt it. Here in Cincinn-apathy, one of the largest plant-ations in the country, many of our people are content with their positions and their status, and they are afraid that if they make waves they will not get that extra ration of biscuits from the *massa*.

But, that's all right. If we get 50% participation, I will be happy. We must put an end to the exploitation of our people and our Holy Days. Get a movement started in your city and help change the economic situation in which we find ourselves.

This Christmas, and every one thereafter, please make it a point to change your purchasing habits. You <u>owe</u> it to yourselves. You <u>owe</u> it to your children. Please don't end up <u>owing</u> it to the merchants. Let's return to our Holy Days. Enough with these "holidays."

Section Six

Our Psychological Illness

Our doubts are traitors and make us lose the good we oft might win by fearing to attempt.
William Shakespeare, *Measure for Measure*

A cat that steps on a hot stove once will never step on a hot stove again ... but neither will it step on a cold one.
Mark Twain

Someone said, "If you keep doing the same thing the same way, you will keep getting the same results." That sums it up for us when it comes to economic empowerment. For the past 35 years, at a minimum, Black people have been played, not only by white people but by our so-called leaders as well. Unfortunately, we continue to play ourselves.

The craze for new prisons is supported by our proclivity to put ourselves in harm's way, thus making ourselves economic slaves to economic pimps. I always say, "They build 'em—we fill 'em," conspiracies and systemic inequities notwithstanding.

Most of our people want economic empowerment, but do not want to make the sacrifices necessary to achieve it. If we want to be the boss, we must be willing to pay the cost.

Each year we hear about "The Dream" of Dr. Martin Luther King, Jr., and instead of making the dream come true, we continue to promote the dream itself. The only way to make a dream come true is to wake up.

Another negative psychological trait we seem to have adopted is the "First Negro" syndrome. You know what I mean. We still have Black people who think because they are the first to be appointed or the first to get a certain job they are somehow "better." When will we ever stop counting to one?

Our psychological illness is grounded in historical "Willie (Lynch) Chip" programming. We cannot afford to continue to lean on that crutch, however, especially when we know better. We must change our minds about one another. Our psychological freedom is the primary ingredient for our economic freedom. We have to cure ourselves.

We Want Substance Without Sacrifice

We have all heard the saying "You can't get some-thing for nothing." We also know that if it looks too good to be true, it probably is. We are familiar with these and other very simple and logical sayings, but too many of us are unwilling to allow them to guide us when it comes to gaining our true economic freedom.

Let's take a look. Black people - at least most of us - understand that, as Frederick Douglass taught us, only through some form of struggle will we achieve our freedom. As for our economic freedom, that truism applies to an even greater degree. If we want economic empowerment we must be willing to sacrifice something to obtain it.

I take you back in recent history to Montgomery, Alabama and the bus boycotts. Sacrifices were made by those who were willing to walk instead of conveniently ride the buses. Those people wanted something of substance and they sacrificed to obtain it.

Fast forward to today. We give a lot of lip-service to wanting our economic freedom, but in many cases we are unwilling to give up even the slightest measure of our "convenient" lifestyle to achieve the freedom we long for. And then if we do manage to make a small sacrifice we want our reward instantly; we want immediate gratification. Further, when we decide we have had enough of being discriminated against, being caricatured, and being treated unfairly we conjure up superfluous attempts to redress those issues.

When we catch someone calling us a bad name, we sue him or her, and we insist they go to sensitivity training. When white radio personalities say things like "black hoes" we sue them because they hurt our feelings, and we ask for a boycott. (By the way, has anyone asked for a boycott of those Black personalities who use similar pejorative terms in their music videos? Just a thought.) When we feel discriminated against by big business or even a small business for that matter, we seek retribution through feeble economic sanctions and we dust off our protest signs and start demonstrating against them.

These solutions are all very nice and have some impact, but when you really look at what we have accomplished with these strategies you see very little long term benefit. For instance, everybody was angry at the high gasoline prices in the spring of 1999. A "Gas-out" day was called over the Internet and in various media. The problem was that it lasted only one day. What would make us think that because we do not buy gasoline for one day we will make the prices go down? How ridiculous to think we could have an impact, especially when the dealers know we will be there in great numbers the next day to "fill 'er up." We needed to sacrifice more than one day without gasoline to have been effective.

Back in the 1980's Revlon made a public *faux-pas*. We boycotted, and after the company hired a Black Public Relations person and made some donations to Black organizations, all was well again. Since then Black people have probably bought more than enough Revlon products to make up for the boycott.

The Texaco incident is another one. After all of the hoopla and all of the money from Texaco's *caught-in-the-act-contingency-fund* was distributed, it was business as usual. Have you seen those beautiful commercials on television featuring Black dancers, sponsored by you know who?

The politician in Colorado who said disparaging things regarding the possibility of George W. Bush losing the Republican nomination (He said a Black woman would have to say he had a relationship with her for Bush to lose the nomination) was asked, no, he was begged, to "apologize." He did. Okay, so what? Okay, now what?

Since some Black employees at Coca Cola cried foul at what they described as discrimination by that soft drink company, our friends at Coke are giving us a chance to win a free trip to be with Tom Joyner and they're donating funds to his scholarship program. In return, "all" they want us to do is collect their bottle caps and turn them in. Need I say more?

We could look at many other examples of our futility and our acquiescence to those that do and say things against us, but we must also look at what we gain from our reciprocal actions against them. From my seat, I can't see much gain, at least not for us. For them, well, that's another story.

Are we tired enough of being manipulated to make the sacrifices we must make to gain true freedom? Nothing of real substance will come to Black people unless and until we are willing to lay something on the line. It's not about what someone calls us; it's about what we answer to. (Besides, what do you think they call us after we accept their "apologies"?). It's not about another Black face on television; it's not about another Black person getting a cushy job; it's not about someone saying "I'm sorry"; and it's not about collecting someone's bottle caps.

It's about economic empowerment for Black people—true freedom. Anyone, friend or foe, who does not move us toward that goal is not working in the best interests of our people. The empty gestures we see by corporations and individuals do nothing for us economically. It's always all about them. Yet we keep going back to them for redress when we find they are insincere. The onus is on us to make the individual and necessary sacrifices commensurate with our dissatisfaction.

When we walk away, let's be prepared to stay away and build our own economic base by paying a little more if necessary and by pooling our dollars. Without that kind of sacrifice we will never have anything of substance.

Frederick Douglass also said, *You don't get everything you fight for, but you fight for everything you get.*

Are You Still Dreaming?

This is the time of the year when Black people reflect on the life of Dr. Martin Luther King, Jr., whose life has been reduced to "Content of our character" and "I have a dream." His speeches will be recanted at celebrations and memorials throughout the country. And, of course, we will hear the statement, *They killed the dreamer, but they could not kill the dream.* Yes, Dr. King will be remembered in many ways, but I venture to say that most of the references to his memory will be framed in "The Dream."

For all the things that he did, it is sad that this man is so broadly characterized as a mere "Dreamer." King did much more than just dream and it would be great if we could give him another, more appropriate moniker. He acted upon his dream on a daily basis. Too often these days we hear so much from our "leaders" about what we should do, but we see very little follow through by them. Some of us should be called "dreamers."

Here is my take on the dreamer and his dream. Three or four years before Dr. King was killed, he placed considerable emphasis on economic empowerment. He began to espouse the notion that civil rights could not be fully realized nor exercised if we neglected to gain economic justice and economic power. Just before he died he was in the process of organizing the Poor People's March on Washington—the beginning of an economic movement. Do you think that's why he was killed?

In 1963 Dr. King told us he had a dream. He probably had the same dream when he died in 1968. But in my opinion, 38 years is much too long for us, the beneficiaries of Dr. King's work, to be dreaming still. I hear all the time that we must not let "The Dream" die. I hear slogans such as, "Keep the Dream Alive." We have sentiments about this dream of Dr. King's that I think would insult him if he could come back to this earth.

I heard nothing in his speech nor in his other yearnings and admonitions to us that indicated we should keep on dreaming. I never heard him implore us to keep his dream alive forever. I think he wanted us to use his dream as a rallying point for action to make his dream come true. In addition, I think he wanted us to take on the fight for economic empowerment and deal with the "emergency" to which he referred. I think Dr. King wanted us to understand the importance of economic power in this country and to turn our attention and resources to that area as well.

So why are some of us still dreaming today? Why are some of us begging our people to keep the dream alive and well? Why have we not realized at least some of the dream by now? Is it easier for us to simply commemorate Dr. King's dream rather than work to make it a reality?

As far as I am concerned, we should not be proud of the fact that the dream is still alive. We should be embarrassed about our collective economic position. After being warned about the results of economic inactivity on our part by Dr. King, as well as by many who preceded him, we are still dreaming of the world Dr. King illustrated in his speeches and in his work.

Dreaming suggests we are either asleep or sitting around gazing into space imagining what can be. That's all right at first, but there are things we must do after we have the dream. Just to keep on dreaming will get nothing done.

I say, we must awaken from our dream and not continue to keep Dr. King's dream alive. The best tribute that we as Black people can give to Dr. King is action—economic action that will propel us into the next century fully prepared to take our rightful place at the table of commerce.

A fitting tribute would be for us to increase our ownership of businesses, from the natural resource to the retail establishment. We could honor Dr. King better by demonstrating our willingness to support one another, by making sacrifices that would pale in comparison to the ones he made, and by cooperating and pooling our resources for our collective economic benefit.

I don't know about you, but I am tired of hearing the same things repeated every year around January 15th.

Thirty-three years after Dr. King was assassinated we are still getting together and reflecting on what he said and dreamed of rather than celebrating the progress we have made on the realization of his work. Yes, things do take time, but 33 years is a little much, especially when you consider the economic impact Black people have on this country's economy.

This year and henceforth, why not make a pledge to act on Dr. King's dream? Wouldn't it be wonderful if we could look back this time next year and see significant change and progress vis-à-vis "The Dream"? If we hold Martin Luther King, Jr. in such high esteem, we should be ready and willing to continue what he started. We should commit to picking up the gauntlet he laid down and pass it on to the next generation.

These are the best ways to commemorate the man who died fighting for us. Breakfasts, lunches, dinners, parades, marches, and candlelight vigils are fine. But if at the end of those functions, Black people do not, for instance, collect five dollars from each participant for a common fund to assist those in need, if we simply write a check to the hotels for using their banquet rooms and eating their chicken dinners, if we march in solemn anguish only to go home and await next year's event, we have done nothing.

It would make no sense for Black people to participate in hundreds, maybe thousands, of functions in the name of Dr. Martin Luther King, Jr. without accruing economic benefit from them. A man who died for justice, unity, economic fairness, and a myriad of other just causes, should be honored by all of us—Black people especially, by "living his dream" rather than "dreaming his dream."

Even more appropriate is the need for Black people to finally pick up on what Dr. King started, to realize what he meant when he said *the emergency we face now is economic,* and to understand that in 2000 "silver rights" are even more important than "civil rights."

So have your celebrations, have your special programs and marches, but while you are participating in them please add some value by implementing one of the aforementioned suggestions or one of your own. Do something that will truly be a worthy tribute to Dr. Martin Luther King, Jr.

To continue to dream and sing "We shall overcome" will not move us to where we need to be. Let's make plans—very soon—to sing "We <u>have</u> overcome" and let's stop dreaming Martin's dream. Let's work on a new dream for our people—an economic dream—and then let's get to work on bringing that dream to fruition.

Economic Slavery – Alive and Well

On December 18, 1865 the 13th Amendment to the Constitution of the United States was ratified. It reads as follows: ***Neither slavery nor involuntary servitude, except as punishment for crime whereof the party shall have been duly convicted, shall exist within the United States or any place subject to their jurisdiction.***

In the case of this particular Amendment, the word "except" carries a great deal of weight. Early in Bill Clinton's presidency he proposed spending some $20 billion on new jails. Prior to him, George Bush was even more gung-ho on the "lock em up and throw away the key" bandwagon.

Now we see that prison-building is at the head of the pack of profitable industries. The stock market is in love with the industry of putting people in jail, and we lead the world in incarcerations. Prison profiteers are busy at prison Expos selling their prison wares and pushing the latest gadgets in the prison industry. Some politicians have even been accused of getting into the act, passing new prison construction and getting a piece of the deal.

Now we hear of new proposals, virtually every week, to use prisoners to perform more and more free labor. They started out making license plates and taking care of the roads. Now some of them are working in prison factories producing items for sale on the outside. The prisoners get 50 cents a day, if that much, and someone else reaps huge revenues from their labor.

Yes, that little word "except" is picking up a lot of steam with prison profiteers and politicians. They are intent on building even more prisons, increasing the number of Black people in jail, and making a killing in the stock market. They want to increase the range of goods and services that prisoners can produce and perform for free ("After all, they are in jail. Why should they be paid a fair wage?").

So, if you are one who brags about the 13th Amendment being the one that prohibits slavery, you are sadly mistaken. The devil is in the details, as they say. And this trend to have men and women, most of whom are Black, work for free is tantamount to slavery prior to 1865. We were prisoners then; we were slaves then; we worked for free; and we were treated terribly.

What then shall we do? I am not one to call for a political rally or a new set of laws to deal with this latest travesty of justice. I have a more immediate solution to the problem. I get letters every week from brothers "behind jail" as Gil Scott-Heron used to say. Most of them say they are locked-up unjustifiably, but some admit they "messed up," they just did something stupid and got caught. Well, the latter group, and those who may be thinking about doing something stupid, are the ones I am addressing. The ones who say they are innocent, while I will not judge them, should pursue their rights vigorously and until they are exhausted.

Those men and women who did stupid things should make a vow never to repeat their stupidity; they must not be a recidivism statistic. Those who are thinking about doing something stupid—well, think about this: Do you want to be a slave? Do you want to be told what to do, when to do it, and with whom to do it? Do you want to continue to create wealth for those who hold you in disdain? If your answer is "No" then turn around now.

We of all people should never allow ourselves to be slaves again, but our men especially are making a beeline to the prisons, filling them up as fast as they can, and the establishment is loving every minute of it. Where else can they rid this country of Black people and make windfall profits from it as well? Man, "What a country," as the Russian comic used to say.

Black men and women, you should know that when you stand in that courtroom, before that judge you have absolutely nothing coming but some time. The best thing and the first thing must be to stay out of harm's way. Stop thinking it won't happen to you, that you won't get caught, because if you do you will become a slave. You will become a pawn in the financial game of prison building, prison maintenance, prison supply, and prison stocks. You will continue to create wealth for others and not for your own people. That is an outrage, and it must change—we must change.

Prison economics is real. We are participating at an unprecedented rate. Let's get smart. Stop the stupidity. Don't play into the hands of the man and his corrupt justice system—you know, the one we always complain about. The best way to stop the injustice is to stay out of the system. More importantly, stop contributing to the wealth of others while at the same time contributing to the new version of slavery.

We don't own any prisons, and we do not control the industry. As a matter of fact, we have virtually no economic stake in it whatsoever. So why are we doing stupid things and going to jail? Why are we increasing the economics of others and decreasing our own? **STOP!**

Remember: Words mean something. The word "except" wields a big stick, especially when it's in the Constitution of the United States. Slavery does still exist in this country, and if you go to jail you will find out first-hand.

Still Counting to "One"

Why is it that each time there is a problem of some kind, something we are unhappy about, or issues we are protesting against, we fall for the "First Negro" game? Albert Cleage taught us about this syndrome back in the 60's and 70's and we are still being duped by it.

You know what I mean. We protest against the dearth of Black involvement in corporate America, and they appoint "The First Black" to the Chicago Stock Exchange. We complain about how unfair our money system is, and they appoint "The First Black" to the upper echelon of the Federal Reserve System. They lull us into a state of euphoria by merely projecting that "The First Black" will become CEO of a major corporation—in two more years.

There are more examples. In our respective cities we still count to one when a new Black fire chief is appointed. We jump for joy when "The First Black" gets the top job on the police force—even in a city that is majority Black. In some areas we still swoon about "The First Black" school principal. I say, "Why has it taken so long?"

It's sad that in this day and age we can still be pacified with "The First Negro" strategy. Our issues are very serious, especially our economic issues. We cannot afford to play into the hands of those who would only throw us a crumb or two to quiet us down. Is "The First Black" being appointed to a position that can really solve our problems? Or, does it merely serve as an isolated symbolic gesture of the sad fact that we can be bought off by window-dressing?

Even more important to me is this: The Federal Reserve System is nearly 100 years old. Should we jump up and down now that a Black man has finally been appointed to a high level position in that organization? The Chicago Stock Exchange has been around for quite some time now. Putting a Black man on the Board in 1999 is really nothing to brag about. Have you ever heard of the okey-doke?

Black people have been putting out fires, policing, teaching, and running businesses since before the end of slavery. Why is it worthy of celebration now that one of us has been promoted to the top spot in anything? The worst part about this is the fact that we play into it. Some of our brothers and sisters would have us believe that because they are "The First Black" to do something it makes them special; they think it makes them better than other Black folks.

If you ask me it's certainly nothing to boast about. Black people have been in this country since its inception. We have participated in its wars, depressions, and its construction. As a matter of fact, we built this country. We have participated in its commerce—no, we were its commerce. What is there to celebrate in 1999 when "The First Black" is appointed to anything? Not much, I dare say. Yet we fall for it every time. And when that does not work, they throw a few Benjamins our way.

Here's the real deal. If we want to celebrate the first Black something, let's celebrate the first Black owned hotel in our town. Let's throw a party when the first Black owned bank is opened. How about doing some bragging about the first Black supermarket in your town? Or, the first Black theater complex, record company, theme restaurant, conference center, or even an airline? Now those are things we can take pride in for being the first.

Let's understand that "The First Negro" principle in 1999 is a prescription for our continued economic enslavement. Those who make it to certain levels and get high appointments, may God continue to bless them and may they do something with those positions to help their people. But, to hedge our bets, we must keep our eyes on what is really important in this country—economic freedom.

Getting caught up in the hype about "The First Black" on a Board, or about anything else for that matter, is not where our attention should be. Sure, rejoice in another brother's or sister's success, but don't revel in the notion that something is being done for our people simply because he or she happens to be the "First."

We have been in this country too long and have committed too much for anyone to still be counting to one when it comes to Black folks. Pardon me for being a party-pooper. But please call me when the number reaches 1000.

Y2K – What Was It Really All About?

In 1997, the term "New Millennium" was the fastest growing and most ominous term in the lexicon. As it loomed before us like the grim reaper, we heard this term used by so many, and we used it in our conversations sometimes as though on January 1, 2000 a magical transformation would take place for Black people and, of course, for the rest of the world.

Well, I don't know about the rest of the world, but other than the possible ramifications of the Millennium Bug, at the rate we were going, I asserted that our brothers and sisters would hardly notice the change—at least economically. We often heard it said that we had to get our economic act together before the next century began. But what if we didn't get it together? What would happen to us? Answer: Nothing plus nothing equals nothing. In other words, if we did nothing, then nothing would happen.

No, there was nothing magical about the date itself, as many implied in their rhetoric. But there was something very scary about the fact that as of December 1998 Black people had made relatively little progress developing collective economic empowering strategies. At that pace, I predicted the year 2000 would not reach our neighborhoods until around 2010.

Status quo is a prescription for failure, and that is especially true for the economic survival of Black people. If we continue down the same economic path we've been on for the past thirty-five years, our movement into and through the New Millennium will mean nothing other than more big New Year's Eve celebrations for Black people. And that would be a shame.

Here is the real deal. Shortly after the turn of the century Black people will go from the second to the third largest group in the United States. Will January 1, 2002, find Black people still owning less than 2% of this country's assets? On that day, will Black families be in last place when it comes to median income and net worth? Will the

New Year enter and find Black people still languishing without a strategy for economic empowerment—and not working on a strategy?

Will our people still be mired in rhetorical ethics discussions about what the government and other sectors of this country should do for us? Will we still place our hope and faith in what Harold Cruse calls *non-economic liberalism*? Will we still have hundreds of "leaders" who are taking us nowhere? Will our youth still suffer the plague of inferior education, fear of being killed by another brother or sister, or not having enough to eat? Will we have learned by then to rejoice in our brothers' and sisters' successes rather than try to bring them down? And will we have learned that we must reach back and help one another once we have "made it"?

Those and other questions are important for African Americans vis-a-vis this New Millennium. They are also vital for consideration today—right now! All the talk about the 21st century, as if it were some measuring rod for our progress, or the lack thereof, was nonsensical and diversionary. Black people surely do not need timelines that give us comfort as we *put off until tomorrow what we can do today.* It was never about Y2K; it's about NOW. The only timelines we should look at are the ones that have passed us by and left our people so far behind the pack.

The question is: What are you doing to help secure a brighter economic future for our children and our families? If each of us would do his or her part to effect positive change in the economic status of Black people, the dreadful doomsday scenarios would not seem as such. I think we are concentrating too much on the destination and missing out on the trip. Where one is going means nothing if there is an accident along the way. Black people suffered a virtual train wreck on our way to economic empowerment back in the 1960's, and we have yet to get back on track.

All of us must ask that question, and we must be willing to admit our shortcomings related to the economic status of our people. Take stock of what you are doing and what you can do to help uplift our people economically. Don't worry so much about the New Millennium; worry instead about the upcoming shopping season. Where will you spend your money? Will you be a participant in economic empowerment or will you be a not-so-innocent bystander cheering the rest of us on from the sidelines?

Will you make every attempt to support your own people, not sometime in the New Millennium, but tomorrow? Will you subscribe to your Black-owned newspapers, support the rest of your Black-owned media, shop at Black-owned stores for artwork, cards, computers, new carpet, music, books, clothing, and everything else you can possibly find in your community that is Black-owned? Will you commit to economic empowerment via your individual action, and sometimes sacrifice, to support your brothers and sisters?

I trust your answers are yes. I also trust you will follow through on your commitment. If the majority of our people do these things—now—the dawning of a new century will mean a great deal to us. But, if we do nothing, continuing our self-imposed economic destruction by giving 95% of all we have to someone else, the year 2000 will come and go as the past thirty-five have—just another insignificant period in the economic saga of Black Americans.

Conspicuous Consumption

Who did you think of when you saw that phrase? It is certainly one that fits the majority of Black people in this country. When I think of spending or consuming by our people I see nearly $600 billion passing from our hands into the hands of folks who do not look like us. I think of the ridiculous notion of our children finding their self-esteem in the names (brands) of persons they would not even recognize if they passed them on the street. I think of our misguided adults who continue to complain about others moving into our neighborhoods and setting up businesses, while we sit around and refuse to do the same thing. I think of our people—Black people—spending, spending, spending, and bragging about how much we spend, as though it were a badge of honor.

Our conspicuous consumption is recorded, documented, and studied by economists and marketers all over the world. Foreigners who come here for the first time know before they arrive who their market is and where they will open their businesses. They know that Black consumers are the primary group from which they can make their fortunes. They know that Black people will allow them—even welcome them—into their communities and buy any-thing and everything they have on their shelves no matter the price. Our conspicuous consumption is a beacon to prospective businesses.

As I walk the streets in my hometown I see our brothers and sisters proudly strutting their stuff. The gold jewelry, the $2,000 wheels for their cars, the "Tommy Gear," the 40-ounces, and all of the other outward manifestations of our collective psychological illness are sad commentaries of our conspicuous consumption. They make it—we buy it. They tell us we will be better athletes—we buy it. They tell us to obey our thirst—we buy it.

Imagine the nerve of department store personnel following Black youth around and characterizing them as thieves—in spite of the fact that these same Black youth spend billions each year—mostly on clothing. Can you perceive millions of Black consumers who cannot wait to take their money to the stores on the day after Thanksgiving and during the Christmas holidays? Those same consumers will struggle for the next year to pay the debts they built up during that time.

Can't you see that by emulating the R.E.A.C.H. Program in Meridian, Mississippi, or doing what the Recycling Black Dollars Program espouses and what the Richard Allen Foundation promotes, following Claud Anderson's Powernomics course, and by practicing the MATAH Network's plan we could turn ourselves around one hundred and eighty degrees? By redirecting a small portion of our consumption spending we can begin to take control of our own future and stop depending on others to provide the very sustenance we need to survive.

Our conspicuous consumption denotes a people in trouble, a people in dire straits, and a misguided people with misdirected values. Our conspicuous consumption is exploited everyday by those who hold us in disdain and even refuse to respect us when we are in their stores spending our money. Our conspicuous consumption causes many businesses to revel "in the Black," which is the only instance that "Black" is used positively by the establishment. Oh yes, they love to be *in the Black* when it comes to their financial statements, and our conspicuous consumption continues to keep them there.

In the Black is where Black people will be if we mount a serious anti-spending campaign and reduce our conspicuous consumption. Currently we are operating at a huge deficit; we are in the red—big time. How do we get out of it?

Think. That's all we have to do to change our buying habits. I contend that if those of us who have a modicum of Black consciousness would simply stop and think before we spend our money, we would make more intelligent purchasing decisions. And please keep in mind that it does not take all Black people to make a change in this regard.

There is a principle known as *critical mass,* which suggests that once a certain point is reached a movement will take on a life of its own.

An excellent example of this is often illustrated by Ken Bridges of the MATAH Network during his presentations. He says that if Black people would simply redirect just five percent more of our half-trillion dollar annual income toward Black businesses, we would reach critical mass and the effort would move on its own, just like a snowball rolling down a hill. When that snowball reaches critical mass you no longer have to push it; the snowball will continue to roll under its own weight.

That's the kind of economic movement we must have in order to change our conspicuous consumption into an effort that will put Black people *in the Black,* provide a solid economic future for our children, and demonstrate once and for all our resolve to take care of ourselves first. Reaching *critical mass* in our own economic movement is *critical* to our economic survival.

Section Seven

From the Mouths of Babes

Black men and women need to create their own economic base. Without economic power there is no political power.
Luther Campbell

Poverty is not about color.
Queen Latifah

As in my first book, I could not write this one without giving some "props" to young people – young people who are practicing economic empowerment principles. I cannot tell you how good it makes me feel to see our young Black brothers and sisters doing what many of our adults just talk about.

We have seen in our young people the drive, dedication, and determination to change the landscape of this country. Two of my favorites are Venus and Serena Williams—not so much for their tremendous abilities in tennis, although I greatly admire that as well, but for their stance on recycling their dollars among Black people.

Using Black sports agents should be the first consideration of our super rich Black athletes. Unfortunately too many of them would rather run directly to the *Jerry Maguires* of the world and give them a significant portion of their salaries. Please give us more Williams sisters.

Then there are young Black entrepreneurs, too numerous to mention, but you will read about some of them in the following chapters. These dynamos are taking care of their business by owning their record companies, their law firms, their clothing companies, and other businesses. They understand what Booker T. was talking about, the admonishments of Marcus Garvey, and the pleadings of Martin Delaney. And they practice those economic principles in their daily lives.

The following three chapters delineate excellent examples of conscious, active, and dedicated brothers and sisters who are creating jobs for their people, hiring Black sports agents, supporting Black businesses, and promoting economic empowerment. Because they are young, intelligent, and affluent they can be the vanguard for future generations. I am proud of them!

You will get a cross-section of initiatives and business ventures being promoted and funded by our young Black entrepreneurs and athletes on the next few pages. Please share this information with your children and your friends, of course.

There has been a lot of talk over the past few years about role models. I do not think there is a better role model, outside of a child's home, than that of a Black entrepreneur.

Many of our children have never even had the opportunity to see an adult get up and go to work in the morning. Many of them have also been indoctrinated on the age-old admonishment to "go to school and get a good job." The young people you read about on the following pages will give those children who follow them a different paradigm regarding entrepreneurship.

Join me in celebrating the accomplishments of our "Young and Relentless" brothers and sisters.

The Young and the Relentless

Economic Empowerment, described by some as the third and final plateau in the evolution of Black people in America, by others as the Civil Rights Movement of the 1990's, is certainly the most discussed topic among African Americans these days. George Fraser, noted networking guru and author, suggests in his latest work, **Race for Success**, that Black Americans are now in the *"...third moral assignment which is to create wealth for Black people and to raise up the poor."*

If Fraser is correct, and most people think he is, who will manage and oversee this "moral assignment" he describes? How will they do it? What will they do to see that Black people move beyond economic rhetoric and trendy slogans to action—goal-oriented, measurable activity that creates wealth? To reiterate—*who* will do these things?

Much of the responsibility for designing and executing the wealth-building process will inevitably fall upon the shoulders of the younger generations. Can they handle it? The blueprints have been drawn by the likes of Frederick Douglass, who said, *When we are noted for enterprise, industry, and success, we shall no longer have any trouble in the matter civil and political rights.*

Booker T. Washington admonished us, *Let us act, before it's too late... before others come from foreign lands and rob us of our birthright.* He also said, *...without [an] economic and business foundation, it is hardly possible to have educational and religious growth or political freedom.*

Marcus Garvey, Madam C.J. Walker, Mary McLeod Bethune, and many other giants of Black history have provided the formulas for economic success. Assuming Fraser's "third moral assignment" began immediately following the Civil Rights Movement, it was the job of the Black *Baby-Boomers* to continue the battle for economic empowerment. But the baton was dropped, and no one has been willing to pick it up. As a matter of fact, Black people kept running without the baton—running after the "opportunity" to eat in lavish restaurants, to buy the best of everything, and to conduct meetings in the grandest hotels.

In others words, the generations of the 40's and 50's failed to finish the race, despite the many brothers and sisters who continued to spread the message of economic empowerment during the 1960's and 1970's. Now it's up to young Black men and women to heed the lessons of the past and shape the economic future of the next generation.

It's going to take people like Carol and Duane Davis, the innovative couple from Winston-Salem, North Carolina who started the Coalition of Black Investors (COBI). It will take the Black MBA's, led by young people like Pamela McElvane, who are concentrating their wealth-building efforts in the banking industry. Likewise, Yvette Lee Bowser, Executive Producer of "Living Single" and other popular TV programs. And it will take more people like 30 year-old Trish Milines, formerly of Microsoft and retired millionaire, who now teaches computing to inner-city youngsters. According to these "new leaders," it's all about economic empowerment.

Forbes Magazine published an article in April 1997, titled *"Badass Sells,"* by Joshua Levine, which aptly illustrates much of the tremendous economic potential within the younger segment of Black America. It also describes how the hip-hop culture has been co-opted by designers such as Hilfiger and manufacturing giants like Nike.

The upside is that within the young Black consumer segment there are those who are changing the economic landscape. What Heavy-D did for Fila and what Grand Puba did for Hilfiger are slowly but surely being reversed. Many young rappers have come to the understanding that it is better to be the producer than to be the consumer. The messages of Booker T. Washington and Martin Delaney have reached these youngsters loudly and clearly.

"If they want some of the flavor, we want some of the meal," says 30 year-old Londell McMillan. He left a New York law firm to start his own law firm and entertainment financing company, according to the Forbes article.

McMillan is raising $100 million to finance projects for his clients, as an owner not an agent.

Then there are others like clothing magnate, Russell Simmons, who also created Def Comedy Jam. There's Brother Shabazz Fuller, a former street vendor who now owns a $5 million clothing company. Everyone knows Spike Lee. But what about 38 year-old Ralph McDaniels and his flourishing clothing venture? How about those recognizable brands like FUBU and Kani, Urbanwear, and Urban Gear? And check out "Da Noise and Da Funk" of Savion Glover and his fantastic Broadway show. This young brother is definitely taking care of business.

All of these examples and many more are evidence of a positive shift in the mindset of Black men and women – young Black men and women learning the lessons of the past, combining them with the reality of capitalism, and making millions of dollars. They are committed to making a profit *from the free market* rather than *being the free market* by refusing to give away their dollars strictly as consumers. Booker T. would be proud.

In addition to the newfound wealth and financial intelligence within the Black music and clothing sector, other young entrepreneurs are busy making headway in their particular fields of endeavor. There's Magic Johnson with his movie theaters and other ventures, and we see other young Black athletes following his lead. They understand that ownership is the key to economic empowerment and wealth-building in Black communities, and they are practicing what many Black "leaders" have only been preaching for decades.

The question now is how will these individual examples of economic empowerment be parlayed into successful strategies that will benefit the masses of Black people in this country? Projected to spend $533 billion in 1999, the paramount objective for Black people must be to move away from the business status quo and become producers, owners, and manufacturers. Again, the instructions have been written and espoused by several men and women, past and present, which, if followed, will lead Black people out of the *economic dark ages* and into the bright light of prosperity.

Dr. Claud Anderson lays out a national economic strategy in his book, **Black Labor, White Wealth**. His main thesis centers on the development of vertically integrated businesses. *To achieve self-sufficiency, blacks must master the principles of capitalism and group economics.* Dr. Anderson continues, *Vertical integration of industries and businesses is a design that has the potential to create numerous individual, but linked businesses, and therefore should become the basis for an economic development strategy for blacks.*

Theodore M. Pryor, author of **Wealthbuilding Lessons of Booker T. Washington**, says the potential power of Black people *...can't be realized to its fullest measure except within the framework of a black economic strategy, which black America has never had or even attempted.* Pryor stresses the need for Black owned businesses to become dues-paying members of at least one Black business organization.

He goes on to say, *Smoke and flames from Black owned businesses do not make measurable contributions to the smog conditions in American towns and cities.* This illuminates another point Pryor makes: *If the Black business establishment disappeared from the American scene this moment, the American stock market would not react one smidgen.*

Pryor's economic strategy for Black people draws upon the biblical experience of the children of Israel while Moses was on Mt. Sinai receiving the Ten Commandments. The people wanted a god to worship, and Aaron allowed them to make a golden calf but warned them they would have to pay a very dear price. They had to make a personal sacrifice first by pooling their gold earrings and other ornaments and tossing them into a common pile for smelting. T.M. Pryor says Black people need a modern Golden Calf.

149

There are several other *voices in the wilderness* promoting their own economic strategies. Most people are familiar with Tony Brown, who has for many years attempted to break through the static thinking of America's second largest population segment. Many people have listened to the acerbic comments and commentaries of Julianne Malveaux, economist, columnist, and television personality. And there is Kelvin Boston, talk-show host and author of **Smart Money Moves for African Americans**. All of these front runners have practical and attainable suggestions for wealth-building among Black Americans.

A relatively new firebrand on the scene, Brooke Stephens, financial advisor and author of **Talking Dollars and Making Sense**, is making even more noise on the subject. She says the two biggest problems for Black people are their attitude and behavior toward money. "African Americans can be so unforgiving in ridiculing each other when it comes to succeeding or failing in business." She asserts, *Many African American dreams of prosperity get lost in suspicion and paranoia.*

Things are about to change. A positive transition is underway. Young Blacks are aware of the fact that all of them will not be the next Dickie Simpkins, much less the next Michael Jordan. Our young hip-hoppers understand the most lucrative jobs are not always on the stage; they can be found in the recording label offices. They grasp the importance of ownership versus being ripped-off by *culture copycats*. And rather than having to choose between the two, as Tommy Hilfiger suggested, young Black entrepreneurs can own a *home and a Rolex watch*—if they want to.

Young Black men and women know the difference between employer and employee. They are fully cognizant of the advantages of producing their own *brands* rather than being *branded* by someone else. Young lions in the Black community are *down with O.P.M.* (other people's money) and they know how to use it to make their own fortunes. Several Black super-rich athletes and entertainers are finally seeing the light and coming to the realization that they only need so many cars, so much jewelry, so many clothes, and so many rooms in their homes. They are finally making some very positive moves in the wealth-building arena.

What do these new developments forecast for this so-called third moral assignment—this new civil rights movement for Black people? A good bet would be that those lessons taught by the men and women of generations past are being followed—finally. Trends indicate that a new generation is stepping up to take on its responsibility and to be accountable for moving Black people forward. By several measures the Black economic *avant-garde* is up to the challenge, having graduated from the school of hard knocks and rip-offs.

Future Black History celebrations should reflect this new thinking and refreshing activity among young African Americans. There must be reverence for the past, yes, and veneration of those who have paid their dues and passed from this earth. But if Black Americans are truly going to move into the next phase of their evolution in this country they must practice, support, and celebrate the economic achievements of their youth. They are indeed making Black History – now.

"Everything must change," as the song goes. According to many young Black entrepreneurs, the change is at hand. They understand that economic empowerment is their earthly salvation, and they know the ultimate precursor for empowerment is control of their resources, whether those resources are intellectual, cultural, or material. As young Turk and star of the hit show *New York Undercover*, Malik Yoba, said in the Forbes article, *Hey man, that's the American way.*

Props to Dikembe

The first chapter in my book is titled, **What's Right With Black People**? It was meant to set the tone for the book and to illustrate the inherent positive, caring, and loving nature of Black people. In that chapter I made the statement: "I love my people." I wanted to make that public declaration so there would be no doubt about my reason for writing the book. And finally, I wanted to illuminate the accomplishments of our people, to show our resiliency, our strength, and our tenacity in the face of the worst treatment ever perpetrated upon a people.

There is a great deal "right" with Black people, and Atlanta Hawks Center, Dikembe Motumbo, is a prime example. This brother is on a quiet campaign to build a hospital in his native country in Africa. Yes, this super-rich Black man is willing to share his wealth with those less fortunate. Yes, this Black man has not forgotten from whence he came and, as a matter of fact, is willing to return and do what he can to help his people.

In a recent interview, Motumbo explained his goal and publicly displayed his determination to continue even if he has to do it all by himself. He scoffs at those who liken him to Don Quixote, those who call his task "too big," and those who only give lip service when it comes to assisting him financially. Dikembe says, "so what?" He continues his quest because he sees a need, is willing to sacrifice to fill that need, and understands the saying, "To whom much is given, much is expected." Maybe his finger wagging is really an admonishment for some of the other players to do better with their resources.

Mr. Motumbo is, whether he wants the title or not, a role model. He is a role model for other super-rich athletes. Just imagine how things would be if each one of those athletes did the same thing he is doing—or, better yet, if they all got together and did one thing. They could build an affordable housing complex in one of our poorest communities, set up a collectively supported endowment for poor children to attend college, or perpetually fund one or two of our Black organizations. There is so much they could do if they worked together.

Sadly, as Motumbo lamented, most of our brothers are not willing to contribute to a collective economic cause. Only three or four others in the NBA have helped him in his effort to raise $49 million for the hospital. And this phenomenon does not merely exist among those who are super-rich. Those of us at the lower rungs of the economic ladder fail to do the same thing.

The super-rich have set records for how many pairs of shoes they can buy at one time (I think the record is $64,000.00 worth). We in the lower economic strata can't wait to pay our next $150.00–$175.00 for the latest pair of gym shoes. Relatively speaking each of us can do better - not only rich athletes but also the rest of us, no matter how much or how little we have. If we would simply reflect on the greatness of our ancestors, their will to live and to provide for us, their progeny, we would do better. If we would consider the benefit of collective economic activity, the potential treasures we could amass for our progeny with all we have in this country today, Black people would surely live up to the greatness that is within us all.

If we would just take a moment to understand the ramifications of virtually giving our resources to others, whether those resources are in the form of agents' fees to whites rather than Blacks, or in the form of patronizing businesses other than our own, we could do better. If we would learn our history, study our culture, and deal with the reality in which we find ourselves—a capitalist society—we could take our capital and create wealth for Black people rather than for everyone else.

There is nothing wrong with self-interest, especially when it is couched in the collective. Self-interest, directed away from our individual desire for superfluous creature comforts and toward others who are less fortunate, will only enhance our individual positions. By giving, we get. By helping, we are helped.

So, give it up for Brother Dikembe Motumbo and others who are doing the same kinds of things for our people. Our greatness demands that we do better. Our very survival in this country demands that we do better. It's not about how many pairs of shoes you have; it's about how many children you can feed, how many businesses you can help build, and how many brothers and sisters you can help educate.

Motumbo is leading the way, and at 7 feet 2 inches he is certainly tall enough for all of us to see—and to follow. Thanks, Dikembe.

Slam Dunk, Touchdown, Homerun, Match – Finally!

Well, somebody had to do it. Somebody had to say enough is enough and stop handing over hard-earned dollars to the *Jerry Maguires* of the world. That somebody, or should I say, those *somebodies* are young Black athletes. And let me be one of the first to say, BRAVO!!

In my book, **Economic Empowerment or Economic Enslavement—*We have a choice***, there is a chapter titled, "**A Pitch for Black Sports Agents**." I discuss the ridiculous reality of Black athletes giving as much as ten percent of their earnings to agents who have no interest in Black people other than what they can get from them. I also strongly suggest that Black athletes "wise-up" and use other Black experts in finance, accounting, investments, and law to take care of their business.

The book, in addition to hundreds of articles in hundreds of newspapers around the country, seemed to have fallen on deaf ears around the various sports leagues. But now the tide has turned. According to a recent article in **Newsweek Magazine**, titled *"The New Color Line,"* Black athletes, young Black athletes are showing the way to true economic empowerment. They are exercising their prerogatives to support their own people, namely, other Black professionals who can do the same things the *Jerry Maguires* can do. Finally, super-rich athletes are coming to the realization that the *Rasputin* of all myths, "The white man's ice is colder," is far from the truth.

I am so overjoyed I can hardly think straight. Talk about a new day, talk about a new awakening, this is the big one. Just imagine. A significant share of the millions of dollars being made by athletes going to other Black professional agents is a milestone that must be repeated hundreds of times over. I hope others, including Black entertainers, will follow the lead of stalwarts like Ricky Williams, who may have been passed over by the Colts because of his "hangin' with the brothas" mentality. You know what I mean; he may have been "too Black."

Keyshawn Johnson, James Bettis, Venus and Serena Williams, Ron Mercer, Vin Baker, Allen Iverson, Ray Allen, Robert Horry, and Charles Woodson, here's to you. Here's to all Black athletes and entertainers who understand the true meaning of cooperative economics. There's nothing wrong with mutual support; there's nothing wrong with sharing your resources with your brothers and sisters, you know, just like other groups do.

Just watch. There will be a clarion call for "fairness" from white sports agents. There will be accusations of "reverse discrimination." But allow me to postulate. If the NBA and the NFL comprised 80% Jewish athletes, the agents would be of that same persuasion. If the leagues were made up of Asian players, Asian agents would rule the day. Likewise for Hispanic players and agents.

Let's not fool ourselves into thinking that what these young men and women are doing is in any way wrong. They are doing what Booker T. Washington admonished us to do 100 years ago. They are doing what many of us only talk about; they are doing what some of us practice only one day per year during Kwanzaa. These trailblazing, strong, dedicated, aware, and conscious young athletes stand tall among us, and I am proud to be a Black man—because of them and others who have taken similar stands.

When I write I often wonder if anyone is reading - if anyone is heeding, if anyone really cares about anything else other than personal accumulation of creature comforts and social status. I wonder if Black people really understand the importance of economic empowerment and if we are willing to do what it takes to achieve it in this country, especially in light of our resources. I wonder if we have the capacity, among all of our material gain, to raise our level of Black consciousness to the point where it becomes a habit to seek out Black businesses with which to spend our money. With what I hope is a growing trend among Black athletes, I believe we do have the will and the ability to do the right thing for ourselves.

We still have some educating and following up to do. For instance, in my hometown the other day, the number one draft choice on the football team hired the top *Jerry Maguire* and shared his $54 million contract with him. Likewise with another one of our "brothas" on the team a few years ago. But that's all right; we'll get it together with the help of the new, avant-garde, fearless, and conscious cadre of Black athletes.

In my book, I also mention some of the "old pros" that opted for Black agents years ago. Thank you for doing your part too. All of you are paragons of what success is all about. I am proud of you. All of Black America should be proud of you as well. And don't forget: The secret to economic empowerment is circulation of dollars. All right, Black agents, it's your turn. Where are you spending your money?

Section Eight

The Enemy Within

The [Negro] race will free itself from exploiters just as soon as it decides to do so.
Carter G. Woodson

Blacks have no balancing social devices that punish those Blacks who sacrifice members of the race for their own personal advantage. Black America is void of social accountability policies and enforcement devices.
Dr. Claud Anderson

From personal experience, I know that organizations, like countries and empires, cannot be destroyed from without, unless they are first destroyed from within.

The same truism applies to so-called Black communities. Thus, the question is: Where should we place our attention when it comes to improving our lives economically?

I contend that we should look inward and begin to purge ourselves of those who would destroy us from the inside out. When I say purge I do not mean physically. I am suggesting that conscious brothers and sisters work together, away from the *Sambos* among us, for economic empowerment.

The enemies among us must not be allowed to participate in our meetings and disrupt them. Our enemies must not be given free passes to insert themselves into "leadership" roles only to lead us down the paths laid out for them by the establishment.

It is one thing to fight the powers-that-be to get our freedom; it is another thing to fight our own people. Keep in mind the army that fights for economic empowerment will not include all Black people. Those of us who are willing to fight without compromise must understand how to identify the enemy—all enemies.

Following are writings that deal with our internal structures, our internal issues, and problems that are germane to us alone. You know, those housekeeping issues that are only for the family to deal with.

As with any family, we have those who are not in sync with other family members. The universal Black family is no different. We must recognize who our enemies are and be willing to face them with our concerns and hold them accountable for their actions.

We must also realize that our enemies come in several forms, cloaked in sheep's clothing, stroking us with condescending platitudes, promises of prosperity, and all the while they are padding their own pockets and neglecting the collective needs of our people.

Keep your eyes open for the enemies within.

Robin Hood? – *Or, just robbin' da hood?*

For too long we have read about Black people who espouse the best interests of the less fortunate and, when held up to the light they turn out to be just the opposite of what they proclaim. For too long now we have seen, lived with, and tolerated those individuals in our communities. You know the kind. They talk a good game but when you take a critical look at what they have accomplished there's simply nothing there—except, deception, rip-offs, and dishonesty—oh yes, and a great deal of personal gain.

The very sad part about this too-often repeated scenario is our willingness and eagerness to accept anything these folks do. Many times we are well aware of their *modus operandi;* we know what they have done in the past and we know what they are going to do in the future, but we just keep on taking what they dish out.

They tell us they are "fighting for our rights, keeping 'the man' honest, and getting us jobs." They say they are making sure the poor people get what they deserve from the well-to-do folks. In other words, they want us to believe they are modern day Robin Hoods. Well, they got the "Hoods" part right anyway.

It's shameful, considering the collective economic condition of Black people today, that there are those of us who cannot see beyond personal, selfish, dishonest gain. It's sad to think we have Black "robbers of da hood" in our community meetings, sitting in our church pews, on our city councils, serving as mayors and congresspersons, and ripping us off via their so-called businesses. I know they have been among us for many years, but nevertheless it's a sad commentary. In many cases they would have us believe they are taking from the rich and giving to the poor. But the poor stay poor and get less, while the "Robin Hoods" get more.

There are those among us who, as commentator Elizabeth Wright says, "...do not want the patient to get well." As long as they have patients they can continue to perform surgery on us, cutting out our vital organs, administering medicine to us that keeps us in a constant state of euphoria, and making many of us believe that up is down and down is up.

What can we do about these "robbers in da hood?" First we must be willing to identify them—to call them on the carpet for their actions and let them know we will not tolerate it any longer. That's a tough one, I know. Because they can be bought, they will surely try to buy some of us. So watch out for the scam. Don't fall prey to accepting a few dollars in exchange for the souls of your people. Don't allow yourself to be inducted into this Hall of Shame; there are far too many *dis-honorees* already.

We must let these robber barons know they are not welcome at our meetings. We must take them aside in our churches and speak to them about their behavior. We must run continuous information campaigns against them, not just when they are seeking office but all year long. And when they commit unethical business practices, when they do not provide the product or service they promise, or when they lie, cheat, and steal, we must not continue to accept it. We must sanction them, not by destroying their businesses but by cessation of our patronage until such time as they get their acts together. If we accept mediocrity, dishonesty, shell games, and flowery speeches from our people, we deserve everything they do to us.

The final reality in this economic conundrum in which we find ourselves is the fact that Black people in the United States are the most educated Black people in the world. As I said in a previous article, "If we are so smart, why are we so far behind?" We are behind, in large part, because despite having all the information we need to change our condition we continue to conduct ourselves as though we are ignorant. As Carter G. Woodson said, however, we are "Mis-educated." The phrase "Ignorance is bliss" must be especially for us. We know better but we are not willing to do better—so, no better for us.

Do an honest assessment of the Black business, political, social, and religious environments in your locale. Many of the problems we face begin and end with us – our people. Only we can deal with them. We complain about "others" coming into our communities and taking without ever returning anything. We must also clean up our own backyards and stop allowing Black people to take advantage of us as well.

After your assessment, make it a point to stay true to yourself and your people by calling attention to the ill-practices of our people—not by your opinion but by your facts. Talk directly to them first about the problem, and then be prepared to take it to the streets if they do not change. Our economic future will be a direct result of our ability to work together in support of one another. In order to do that we must have standards for ourselves as well as for others. We cannot allow the self-proclaimed Black Robin Hoods to continue Robbin' da Hood.

The Stockholm Syndrome

We learned in our history classes that during World War II many prisoners-of-war took on the characteristics of their captors. Of course it was not the first time in history that phenomenon occurred. The same kind of thing happened during slavery, when some of the slaves were put in charge of other slaves—to watch them and report on them to the slave master. There were even more examples of this during other wars and conflicts.

What does this have to do with economic empowerment of Black people? Well, today the same syndrome exists in our people. Many of us have seen it up close and personal—including myself. The problem in Y2K is that Black people are not slaves, yet we conduct ourselves as though we are, especially when it comes to economics. Some of our people have taken on the characteristics of slave masters and continue to watch over their master's spoils, while others of us stand by, watch it happen, and say (and do) nothing.

The Stockholm Syndrome reminds me of a book I read in high school called, "Animal Farm." It described a situation on a farm where all of the animals complained about how they were being treated by the farmer. The animals wrenched control of the farm from the farmer, and the pigs, who were perceived as the smartest, began to take over.

After the pigs had been in charge for a while they began to take on the same characteristics as the farmer about whom they had complained. Then the other animals began to complain about the pigs because the pigs thought they were entitled to more privileges, more food, more liberties, and such.

Black people, unfortunately, suffer from this kind of activity today. Certain Blacks think of themselves as privileged, not when compared to white people but when compared to their own brothers and sisters. They perceive themselves as "better," smarter, and on a higher level than their less fortunate brothers and sisters, which plays right into the hands of their oppressor.

In my hometown, we have a quiet and informal system that keeps Black people "in their places" and perpetuates a dearth of economic empowering projects in so-called Black communities. Whenever there is an appointment to be made, the same Black persons get the call. Whenever an opinion is needed for the media, the same Black persons get quoted. Whenever the establishment decides to share some of its wealth by giving out contracts, you guessed it, the same small cadre of Black companies get the deal.

The worst part about this kind of control by whites and acquiescence by Blacks, who incidentally make up nearly 50% of the population of Cincinnati, is the fact that whenever Black people get a foothold and begin to build a foundation for economic empowerment, it is destroyed. Sadly, our organizations and institutions are destroyed from within by Black people who, in many cases, are sent by white people. As disturbing as it sounds, we are our own worst enemy when it comes to economic empowerment. Talk about the Stockholm Syndrome and Animal Farm; we are living examples of both.

Some of our brothers and sisters are so entrenched in their own individual "perceived power" (I say perceived because it is not really power) that they are willing to keep their own people down, sometimes by walking on them, just to please the establishment and soothe their own egos. That is sad.

What does this say about us as a people? It says first of all that we still have a long way to go to get our true economic freedom. It says that some of us have opted for economic enslavement rather than economic empowerment. It says that some of our brothers and sisters are willing to sell their souls for a few dollars or for a board appointment or for a political position.

For me it says that those of us who are ready and willing to move in concert and make the sacrifices necessary for economic empowerment must move ahead and leave behind the slaves who want to stay on the plantation. I am not saying we should forget about them, but we must move on and build our own economy. Some of them will get on board later—others will never come along.

We will probably always suffer from the Stockholm Syndrome and be victims of those "Black pigs" who think they are privileged and work to suppress the rest of us, thus achieving the very same goals of the farmer. But we must find likeminded brothers and sisters and move with them, because it never takes the entire group to accomplish a goal. It's the "80-20 Rule"—you've heard of it.

So if you are suffering from the Stockholm Syndrome, please get some help. If you are a privileged pig on Animal Farm, please understand that you still have to march to the tune of the farmer. The rest of us, who know who we are and are willing to do what we must for our futures, let's work together in support of one another. Let's pool our resources and build our own institutions and businesses, and let's take control of our communities.

If we are prisoners, the bars are only in our minds. If we are farm animals, our containment is merely psychological.

Economic Exploitation

There is an intersection in my hometown that has a rent-a-center, a pawn shop, and a check-cashing outlet on three of the four corners. Ironically, on the other corner there is a bank. Every time I drive by I think about the money being wasted by Black people and the money being made by others via those businesses.

Of course these establishments are always found in Black neighborhoods and in most instances owned by someone other than Black people. Have you noticed the commercials for a national chain of furniture and electronic rental stores? One features a Black family, in which the father is hugging a television. The other one shows an Hispanic woman with her child ecstatic because they are finally going to get the furniture they always wanted.

What they are going to get are usury interest rates. What they are going to get along with their "no down-payment" and "no credit check" is the convenience of paying a ridiculous amount each week for a piece of furniture or a stereo unit. They are all smiles on the commercial, but they wouldn't be smiling if they knew they were paying as much as 520% annual percentage rate on that precious television.

Things have gotten so bad, and probably embarrassing for the regulators, that new laws are being passed to stop the mass rip-offs of unwary consumers, the vast majority of whom are poor. Limits are being placed on interest rates to slow the bloodletting just a bit.

The pawn shops. Well, we know the deal there. They have been in Black and poor neighborhoods forever, and they are just as profitable now as they were thirty years ago—maybe even more. The gold and diamonds and video cameras and watches are still in high demand and are still being moved by our people at a very profitable rate.

The new kid on the block, the check-cashing outlets and instant lending establishments, are making a killing as well. They make convenient "payday" loans and will graciously cash your check, for a few percentage points that is. These places are popping up all over our neighborhoods. Most of them, as well, are owned by other ethnic groups. The check cashing game preys on the poor and the ignorant, and the owners are reaping untold harvests.

As I said, the irony is that a bank sits on the other corner. Oh yes, it can be placed in the same category in some respects. Don't forget about those $27.00 returned check charges and those 20% interest rates on their credit cards. Man, it's Christmas time all year long for these guys.

We don't even need to pose the question, "Why are these establishments so prevalent in Black and poor neighborhoods?" It's quite obvious why they are there. A more suitable question is "Why are we their primary customers?" Is it because we have no other alternatives? Is it because of our instant gratification mindset? Is it because we don't trust banks? Is it because our needs are so immediate that we are willing to sacrifice a portion of what we have—a major portion—to satisfy those needs?

Whatever the reason, I hope we will make a concerted effort to cease and desist this kind of business activity. We cannot afford to patronize these businesses nor should we patronize them. They are leeches and bloodsuckers of the lowest form and we should stay away from them at all cost. They only make it easy for us to avoid responsibility, to put off planning, and to always stay behind when it comes to economic empowerment.

We must change our habits and our thinking when it comes to our money. Why give it to someone else for something you don't need or can wait a little longer to have? Why pay outlandish rates to obtain some temporary creature comfort, especially if that item is not going to help you earn money in return? It makes no sense for us to practice consumerism the way we do. Of course, the money-changers love it and are laughing everyday as they make their way to their bank steeped in the confidence that come tomorrow, bright and early, one of us will be standing at his front door when he arrives to open his shop. They know us like a book. Don't they?

By the way, the adjoining blocks of that intersection I spoke about also sport a Korean hair products store, the proverbial Korean wig shop, a dingy five and dime store, a major supermarket and drugstore with police guards, and a sprinkling of other little places where Black consumers can dish out their money.

There are improvements and changes being made, however. A group of Black doctors bought one of the buildings and is currently renovating the property and bringing a new enterprise to the neighborhood. Just down the street our Black Chamber of Commerce recently purchased a building for our headquarters. And one of our oldest Black owned businesses is one block away from us.

While all is not gloom and doom, more of our income is still flowing out rather than staying in our neighborhoods via those "convenient money stores" and other non-Black businesses. If we could just get to the point of delaying our purchases and pooling our resources, we could enjoy the convenience of ownership and self-sufficiency—and the money-changers would leave the next day.

Section Nine

It's Not Personal.
It's Just Business.

Without a doubt, the best way for us to accumulate wealth quickly and increase the circulation rate of our dollars within our community is through the rapid formation of businesses within our community.
Robert Wallace

The propensity to truck, barter, and exchange one thing for another ... is common to all men, and to be found in no other race of animals.
Adam Smith

We are an emotional people; I think most of us will agree on that. However, we often allow our emotions to control our actions or the lack thereof.

For example, we patronize stores in our neighborhoods, stores owned by "other folks," and complain about those same folks calling us names and selling inferior products to us.

We get mad when we hear that someone called us the "N" word and we insist they apologize—before we go back to them to spend our money. What a deal, huh?

We reach a fever pitch when we hear speeches and sermons, and then we walk away and do nothing. We get mad at corporations, march and protest in front of their businesses and even boycott them, but we fail to do our due diligence when it comes to following through with something for ourselves. Instead, we go home and await the next crisis.

This country was founded for economic reasons and has operated that way ever since. Unless we are planning to make a mass exit, we had better start taking care of our business. We must not allow our consumption spending to be exploited by those who hold us in disdain. We cannot afford to allow economic predators to run rampant in our neighborhoods. We must value our Black Market and learn how to use it to our advantage—not everyone else's.

Black (?) Hair Care Products

(Note: In retrospect, it turns out that this case was a harbinger of things to come. Carson, Pro-Line, B.E.T., etc.)

The latest in a significant chain of economic events affecting Black people is the purchase of Soft Sheen Products, a Chicago-based Black hair care producer. Of course this incident in and of itself is not earth shaking and will not cause Black people to start jumping out of windows. However, it does recall haunting memories of the mid-1980's and Irving Bottner, the *Rascal of Revlon.*

Bottner, then a high-ranking executive at Revlon, predicted Black hair care companies would be taken over by white companies in about 15 years. He made that statement sometime in 1985. Well, here we are 13 years later, and after Johnson Products bit the dust in 1992, Soft Sheen has now been captured—by a white-owned company. (At last check Johnson Products is now in the Carson camp, a Black-controlled company.)

Back in the mid-1980's, when the American Health and Beauty Aides Institute (AHBAI) was established, Bottner's arrogant (and some said outlandish) statement started a national boycott of Revlon products. Remember how we stopped buying Revlon and paraded in front of coffins and laid our Revlon products to rest? We were symbolizing the death of that line in our community. Surely you remember how we swore that was the final straw. There would now be grave retribution for Revlon and its insolent executive. Yeah, right.

Now we have seen the sale of two of our landmark companies—two companies started and managed by Black brothers and sisters. These companies provided jobs for Black people, were domiciled in Black communities, and stood as paragons of entrepreneurial tenacity and savvy for Black youth. While I will not concede to Bottner's prediction as having been fulfilled, I will concede to our continual *sleeping at the wheel* when it comes to what is happening to Black people economically.

After we ranted and raved about Revlon's *faux pas* and promised never to let them off the mat, Revlon went into its *caught-in-the-act contingency fund* and began damage control in the Black community. Contrition was in great supply and apologies were had all around. Black people acquiesced again, and the rest is history. We were back to business as usual in the Black community. We made them pay all right, and they are still paying, only this time they are paying for Black owned businesses.

A 35 year-old, nearly $100 million Black owned company, and leader among Black hair care firms, Soft Sheen has now become the property of L'Oreal, a Canadian conglomerate, in what the New York Times calls a "...bold move to become the world leader in ethnic beauty..." How did this happen? Or maybe a better question is, "Why did this happen?"

The sale of Soft Sheen and other Black-owned firms, Bottner's comment notwithstanding, is merely a sign of the times. In the merger-charged atmosphere that abounds in this country everyone seems to be forming partnerships and alliances except Black people. Thus our companies are being devoured by the highest bidder. There is a literal feeding frenzy for the Black dollar. Black people are throwing our dollars to the sharks, and they are getting fat and happy at our expense. The sad part is we continue to do so, even after being insulted by those who benefit from our dollars.

We can see the same thing happening along the continuum of Black hair care with the distributors and various suppliers, mostly Asian, controlling the prices we pay for products manufactured by Black people for Black people. We also see the trend in the Funeral Industry as well as in the music business. Is it a good thing or a bad thing?

As one of the leading authorities on the Black hair care industry, Lafayette Jones, puts it, "The sale of companies like Soft Sheen can have positive and negative ramifications. On one hand, the opportunities I had to work as Vice-President in some of the leading Black hair care firms in this country would probably not have been available had they not been owned by Blacks." Jones continued, "Jobs in our community and entrepreneurial examples for our children to emulate are vital, and so too is corporate ownership. However, it is a business decision, in light of our current economy, and how the Gardner family (founders and owners of Soft Sheen) chooses to parlay its 35 year investment in the company."

"My sincere wish," said Jones, " is that L'Oreal will simply do the right thing and continue to be a good corporate citizen, just as the Gardner family was—especially on the south-side of Chicago. If that occurs, the sale of this Black business will not be perceived as a negative deal."

So what will we see from this latest sale of the largest Black hair care business to a white owned company? Are we witnesses to the continuous erosion of Black economic infrastructure? Or, are we on a new path of alliance and partnership vis-a-vis our global economy and the battle to control the largest share of a particular market?

What we as Black people can do—no, what we must do, is stay vigilant. Watch the results of this deal and be prepared to withdraw our support (our dollars). If L'Oreal management turns out to mimic Revlon executives who recently fired many of its top-level Black employees, then we must take reciprocal action. This time we must not simply threaten, we must not simply march and demonstrate, and we must not be temporary in our protest. This time our economic retribution must be swift, certain, and very long term.

If we are not going to own businesses in this global economy, we must make those whom we support account-able for the billions of dollars we provide them. Soft Sheen is only the tip of the proverbial iceberg. What about Black-owned radio and Black-owned newspapers? Are we prepared to lose those too?

Consumer Awareness - A Growing Phenomenon?

Yes! More and more consumers are educating themselves on the value and power of their dollars. An increasing number of consumers, especially Black consumers, are making conscious informed decisions on where, when, how, and with whom to spend their hard-earned money.

Many Black consumers are well aware of their particular impact on this country's economy vis-a-vis spending power. They are also quite knowledgeable of the percentage of purchases they make within various industry categories. This "new thinking" consumer buys or refuses to buy certain products on the basis of rational business practice: Reciprocity.

A good business relationship is symbiotic—mutually dependent, mutually satisfying, and mutually beneficial. Today's consumer is looking for value, quality, convenience, availability, choice, and a new shopping item—*quid pro quo*. For instance, when I shop, if there are just a token few items in a small isolated space on the shelf, even if the store has what I want, I will not buy it or anything else. That's because, as a consumer, it makes me feel like an afterthought. I may go into a store for several items but if I am dissatisfied about one of them, the store loses a multiple sale and sometimes a return visit.

Educated consumers want the attention they deserve. They want to know they count, that their dollars count for more than just the pleasant sound of a ringing cash register.

Black consumers want to see more than just one or two of the products they use. They want to know that the next time they come to a particular store the items they desire will be there. In other words, they want reciprocity in the marketplace. Gone are the days when retailers can simply take certain consumer segments for granted. Retailers must be accountable, they must be courteous, and they must be competitive.

With the advent of Minority Chambers of Commerce, especially the more than 300 African American Chambers across the country, educated consumers are flourishing. Chambers are inviting individuals who do not have businesses to join their ranks. Seminars and workshops on Consumerism are being conducted by Minority Chambers of Commerce to enlighten all of their members on the importance of being aware consumers and to drive home the fact that each of us plays a role in this nation's economy.

Buying and selling, that's what it's all about. There's nothing complicated about that. Retailers have known it all along. Now it's the consumers' turn. Aware consumers can be partners or they can be adversaries. For retailers, the former is the obvious choice. With a spending power of $1 trillion, according to the Selig Institute at the University of Georgia, minorities command respect from retailers and should be dealt with accordingly.

Retailers must think differently, if they have not changed already, about the way they treat Black and minority consumers and about the products they offer these market segments. They must aggressively compete for their business and build relationships with their customers that make them want to return to their business to buy again and again. Isn't that how good business is done? I once heard a drugstore owner say his favorite sound was his door chime. When he heard it, that meant a new customer was coming in, an old customer was coming back, or a satisfied customer was leaving.

One trillion dollars makes quite a large pie. You can decide how big your slice will be, Mr. or Ms. Retailer, simply by taking care of your consumers.

The Black Market

Remember the time when that term conjured up all sorts of dreadful notions? I never thought I would see the day when the Black Market would be referenced in a positive vein. Did you? Well that day has come. Everyone, it seems, is discovering the Black Market these days and the President of the United States is leading the way.

On tour across the country in 1999, visiting places like East St. Louis, Watts, and even Appalachia, although the media would make you think there were no Black people living in those hills and hollows, Bill Clinton suggested that marketers should rethink this Black Market thing.

I have heard corporate executives refer to the Black market as the "new emerging market" or the "new urban market." They are rapidly positioning themselves (again?) to take full advantage of this new phenomenon—this new Black Market.

Two questions: Since when has the Black Market been a new market? How is it possible for a market that ranks somewhere between the eighth and tenth largest economy in the world to be an emerging market? It seems to me that this "new emerging" market has been here for quite some time.

So what's all the fuss about? Why are so many folks suggesting that now it's time they take a look at the Black Market? It's time they make some inroads and develop relationships with this Black Market. It's time they realize there's "gold in them there ghettos."

If you ask me, this notion of "discovering" Black people and their spending capacity is yet another foray into the world of economic trickery and diversionary tactics by those businesspersons who have exploited the Black Market for years and want even more from it now. It is insulting for some to suggest that we Black people, with our $500,000,000,000, comprise an emerging market.

The fact is that corporate marketers have known for many years what our spending habits are, what we prefer to buy, when we buy the most, how we make our purchases, and everything else about us as consumers. They have known for quite some time that the Black Market is the market of choice for their products and services. They have been well aware of the fact that they can create advertising and marketing campaigns that will garner billions of dollars from our pockets—with minimal reciprocity on their parts.

Believe me, they know. And to suggest otherwise is a mere sham.

The problem is that we do not have a full awareness of these facts. The other problem is that those of us who do have the facts do little to change the situation. So now we see another marketing and public relations campaign being rolled out that makes us think someone in corporate America is listening to the people in Watts and East St. Louis. The Watts riots were in 1965, folks. Why has it taken so long?

Don't be hoodwinked into believing these people are now interested in our economic wellbeing. They are interested in what they have always been interested in—MONEY—OUR MONEY. You may see a new store (owned by someone other than a Black person) or a new insurance company in your neighborhood, but don't be fooled. Don't be lulled to sleep in economic never-never land by window-dressing. As a matter of fact, pay no attention to it.

Here's a better idea. Form local investment clubs to purchase your own stores and franchises. Now that really would be an emerging market. If the new businesses do move in and show some level of altruism, let their generosity result in something being owned by a Black person or a Black group. Don't let them off the hook by allowing them to merely give you another outlet through which your money will flow—out of your neighborhood.

The economic uplift of our people will not come because corporations bring "loss-leaders" to our neighborhoods. True economic empowerment will come to the Black Market when we understand that we are a potential economic force in this country, when we practice—everyday—some form of cooperative economics, and when we say once and for all, "Our dollars will not be taken for granted."

Let's start being a real Black Market—not a Free Market, which means no one has to pay for it, we just give it away. Let's stop falling for the hype, the public relations, the photo shoots, and all the other things that are done to pacify us. Let's take charge of our Black Market, and if someone wants to buy from it, make them pay!

Empty Victories

When the CompUSA boycotting, letter-writing, faxing, protesting, rationalizing, explaining, apologizing episode in our lives mercifully came to an end, I heard brothers and sisters calling in on the radio, shouting things like, "We won!" and "We brought them to their knees!" and asking Tom Joyner to play, "I'm Black and I'm Proud." I could hardly resist the temptation to call in and request him to play another James Brown song that says, "Let's get together and get some land."

The Computer Wars ended and many of us were celebrating. Many of us were sending in our receipts for our discounts. Even more of us were saying it's safe to go back into the water now. After all, the shark has been killed. The enemy has waved the white flag. We are the victors and we get the spoils. Let the Christmas shopping begin!

While I hesitated to even mention the name of the company, because I did not want to give them more free publicity, I think it's important for you to know the incident to which I am referring. As I followed the chain of events I kept asking myself, "How easily will this one get off?" and, "What will Black people gain from this latest furor?"

The results came in; we celebrated, and could now go home and sit and wait for the next crisis. The infamous company could go back to business as usual and make even more money than it did before this event. We could get our ten-percent discounts and they would get more business. And all they had to say was "I'm sorry."

Sure, they gave some money to a Black owned ad agency and created some slick advertisements for television, like Denny's and Texaco have done. But that was a small price to pay. As I always say, they simply dip into their **caught-in-the-act-contingency-fund** and pay out a few dollars. What a deal!

Here is the real deal—once again. Rather than getting hung-up and bent out of shape about that company, despite the erroneous information we were getting, the time and money we expended doing what we did "against" that company could have been spent "for" our own people. I always say we should not use our precious time and dollars trying to "hurt" someone else; we should use them to "help" ourselves.

I don't want anyone's discounts. I want to buy computers from Black people. If that company wants to give something back, let them put $1 million or so into a Black capital fund for investment in new and established Black owned computer businesses.

More slick advertisements on television, yes they're nice and they helped pay some of the bills at a Black ad agency, but most of that profit goes to the television networks anyway. No benefit to the Black masses there. Apologies? They can keep them. What good are they to us? Haven't we had enough of them anyway? Now they are even using this apology game against us. Jesse Helms demanded an apology from Carol Moseley Braun for protesting against the Confederate Flag. What a joke.

Empty victories are occurring so frequently these days; they are mesmerizing us. We actually believe we have won something. But the other side always wins because of our relentless quest to take our money to their businesses. It matters little that they get caught doing or saying something bad about us (whether it's true or not). We still end up getting mad, ranting and raving, demanding what we call retribution, and then going back to them after a short period of time. Who has the victory in that scenario?

Even more ridiculous is the Black Elf issue in Keebler Cookie advertisements. A spokesperson for the company said the addition of the Black Elf was not in reaction to the lawsuit against his firm. He said it's merely a reflection of what our society is becoming. Well, duh! Did Black people just arrive in this country? (The last time I checked we were here from the jump.) Or, is it just that they have not noticed us until now? Pul-eese, give me a break.

If we are serious about these kinds of incidents, why can't we simply withhold our money for good? Why must we always give them a way out, a way to get back in our good graces? Is it because we are such a forgiving people? Is it because we just like the convenience they provide us by offering all of those goodies they sell in their stores? Or, is it because we just don't want to see a brother or sister with a business that does well?

We made some errors in that economic episode. The initial information received was bogus (Watch out for those "Urban Legends and Myths" on the Internet. Better check them out first) and the results were embarrassing. However, in past incidents we saw the same brand of mismanagement when it came to the negotiations and what we gained from them. If we do not have the right people at the table we will probably come up short, as we have in the past.

From now on, when there are issues like these, let's call on those who deal with them every day of their lives. Before we proceed, let's call Dr. Claud Anderson and Bob Law of the Harvest Institute; call Ken Bridges and Al Wellington of the MATAH Network. Let them negotiate the deal. They are working on projects that benefit the Black collective and they will reap maximum benefits for our people—no matter what ABC or anyone else says.

What the heck, call James Brown; he's been telling us how to handle these situations for years.

Whom Do We Owe?

This shopping season has come to a merciful end, and it is vitally important for us to take stock not only of what we celebrated but how we celebrated as well. Most of us celebrated last "holiday" season by spending our money on gifts. Most of us celebrated by over-eating, over-drinking, and over-indulging in the reveling and hoopla associated with that time of the year. But at a time in our history when Black people earn some $500 billion yearly, 95% of which goes to businesses other than our own, we have a special obligation to change our mindset and that of our children vis-a-vis "Christmas."

We must assess our economic situation and determine whether we are truly good stewards of our financial blessings. If we are not taking proper care of what we have been given by God, our financial blessings will cease. Black people in the United States are known for buying what we want and begging for what we need. That is a prescription for failure when it comes to getting our children to understand the true meaning of economic empowerment in a capitalistic society. We must change our attitudes and our actions regarding our vast collective resources.

In addition, we must work with our children and our young adults to help them see the economic futility of chasing after "brands" and finding their self-esteem in the names of other people such as Hilfiger, Karan, Old Navy, Nike, and the rest. We must teach our children the nuances of economics and admonish them not to make the same mistakes some of us made when we were growing up. Teach them that the Christmas season, or any other season is not a time for them to throw caution - and their money - to the wind.

Simply put, we must reconsider what holidays are all about. They are about M-O-N-E-Y. Our Money. We must learn to keep more of it. We must learn to take better care of it. We must learn to advance and promote our own causes and interests with our money. And we must commit to monetary discipline, not allowing our dollars to be siphoned off by commercialized "seasons," holidays, and other man-made economic windfalls. When we change our direction and our attitude regarding economics and money management, we will finally and deservedly take our place at America's table of economic empowerment.

During Christmas Holidays, and all other holidays and seasons henceforth, remember the importance of stewardship. Remember what these holidays really mean. Please do not take the attitude of the young sister I saw on the news during the last Thanksgiving weekend. So excited about going shopping the day after Thanksgiving, she proudly proclaimed, "I have saved all year for tomorrow. I can't wait to go shopping." It was truly sad to watch, but I understood her attitude towards spending her money. She perceived her spending as a reward for her hard work all year. But what she was really doing was rewarding the merchants.

Now she and many others of us are regretting spending too much, and we will pay for it all year long – and beyond in many cases. Instant gratification has been the economic downfall of many Black people. We want it now, and we will do whatever it takes to get it now. Marketers and salespeople are well aware of our buying habits and are already gearing up for another holiday campaign during which they hope to reap the benefits of our dollars once again. How about we let them down this year?

Please think long and hard about your financial activity this year. We cannot afford to dole out our money, especially to those who do nothing for us in return. We must hold on to what we have and take a stand for economic prosperity—collective economic prosperity—before it's too late. Let this *Y2K* find us with a new economic attitude, one that will move us to a higher economic plateau in this country. We owe it to our children—we owe it to ourselves. Let's not owe it to the merchants.

Ownership - You Call the Shots

All this talk about the media and how it is treating or mistreating Black people is really getting to me. I hear complaints about what is on television and how we have been "dissed" by not being in the shows airing this season. Black movie stars rail against the lack of meaningful parts for themselves in major movies and how they have little if no say-so in the film making business. I hear my people complaining about the dominant daily newspapers' portrayals of Black people. And I hear, almost on a daily basis, how we are being negatively characterized on radio talk shows.

On the other side of the coin, I haven't heard many Black people asking us to simply turn the television off, stop buying movie tickets, and turn to more important things – like building our own economic base in media.

There is a dearth of Black ownership in the film industry despite many of our Black stars residing in the "super-rich" neighborhood. The market penetration rate for white owned newspapers, at least in my city, far exceeds that of the local Black owned newspaper. And talk shows on Black radio are few and far between; they are also very difficult to keep on the air because of a lack of advertising revenue.

So here are the questions. Why are we complaining about white-owned television stations not including us in their programming? Why are we upset about the lack of Black stars in films and the void of ownership in the film industry as a whole? Why are we sulking about white-owned newspapers writing negative articles about us? And why do we lament the state of Black talk shows?

All of the answers are found in the overriding fact that media moguls do what they do, first, because they own the media outlets, plain and simple. And if you have kept up with the news about advertising on Black owned radio stations and other Black media, you know why Black talk shows are suffering. To put it bluntly, we are complaining about "someone else's stuff." If we owned these media companies and large corporations we could call the shots.

I know the first thing some will say. "Well, Bill Cosby tried to buy a television station and they would not sell it to him." So what? At least he tried, and besides, I don't hear too much complaining from him. So we do not own the major television outlets; we also do not have to watch them, especially if we don't like their programs.

Hollywood? Well, as I hear some of the Black stars deride the absence of Blacks in the boardrooms, their roles in films, and the money they make compared to white movie stars, I still see them rubbing against their counterparts at the Oscar presentations. They do this in spite of the fact that only a few Blacks have received Oscars in the history of the award. Some of our Black stars look like they are just happy to be in the room—to be assimilating, if you know what I mean.

The newspaper situation is very strange. We complain about what is written about us and continue to purchase the newspapers. What's up with that? Why would you purchase something from someone (anyone—Black, white, or otherwise) who treats you disrespectfully? Why would you not, instead, buy Black owned newspapers? The same holds true for Black magazines and other periodicals.

Black talk shows are few in number because as long as we keep singing and dancing the establishment is happy. Let us start talking to one another, especially about something important like economic empowerment, and another Black owned station is bought by a conglomerate. Let us start talking and the advertising revenues drop precipitously.

Here's another question. If we want these situations to change, what are we willing to do about them? Demonstrate? File lawsuits? Consider this option. How about we move to own "our own stuff?" How about us supporting our own media to the degree that our Black businesses (and individuals) spend more advertising dollars on Black radio, in Black newspapers and magazines? Now that's an interesting concept. Black owned businesses advertising in Black owned media, strengthening them so they can run the kinds of programs and articles we want to see in addition to creating more jobs for our people.

How about Black stars getting together to invest in their own movie company while, simultaneously, Black consumers start turning off the insulting programs we are complaining about now? Why keep on complaining about other folks' stuff? Just stop buying it.

We will surely see this recent storm develop into some kind of diversity issue or result in someone or some organization being paid to kiss and make up. The "big four" television companies will capitulate and throw in a few token Black characters. We will be pacified and go home to watch television until the next crisis comes along. The media moguls will continue to make their billions from us and we will continue to laugh, sing, and dance. What a trade-off!

I do hope we will consider other options to deal with this latest crisis. We don't need them to pay us off; we do not need their condescending tokenism; and we certainly can do without those shows and films they offer us. But the bottom line is this: It's not about arguing with others about their stuff. It's about obtaining, supporting, and controlling our own stuff.

Section Ten

Our Collective Struggle

If one is continually surviving the worst that life can bring, one eventually ceases to be controlled by a fear of what life can bring; whatever it brings must be borne.

That man who is forced each day to snatch his manhood, his identity, out of the fire of human cruelty that rages to destroy it knows ... something about himself and human life that no school on earth ... can teach.

James Baldwin

Another one of those overused words, I admit. But we have and still do *struggle* to change our collective economic status. We are constantly embroiled in skirmishes on all fronts.

Our struggles, while they may be continuous, must also be collective. If we fight together, in support of one another, I am sure we will overcome our struggles one by one.

Our mistake in some cases has been our propensity to get so involved with the struggle itself and allow it to be our sole focus. Too often we get caught-up in the moment and immerse ourselves in an attitude of struggle. We tend to make the struggle itself the cynosure—the *cause celebre* of our people. We make it such a vital part of our psyche and forget about the end-game.

Some folks just like a good fight, and certainly we need those brothers and sisters who are willing to get into the fray. But we also need those among us who are strategists and planners. We must have persons who can execute projects—projects which become the end result of our struggle. Otherwise, what is our struggle all about?

Check out this section and see if you agree with the premises therein. We have a sufficient number of struggles; we must have more victories.

You Call This Reparation?

A group of Black Americans was recently introduced to the world of reparations from the Federal Government. Black farmers finally achieved a settlement in a case that began in 1983 during the Reagan administration. Oh yeah, that's also the same year the U.S. Office of Civil Rights was disbanded.

Awaiting final approval in March, the protracted lawsuit of the USDA has resulted in 3,000 Black farmers getting "tax-free" payments of $50,000.00 each. Their government debts, which average $87,500.00, will also be 'forgiven" as part of the agreement. I think the forgiving role is reversed. After all, many of those debts were incurred because of the government's discriminatory practices. So who would really be doing the forgiving?

The lawsuit was filed because federal officials unfairly denied loans and subsidies to Black farmers. Let's see now, $50,000.00 for 14 years (1983-1997), comes to just under $3,600.00 per year. Divide that by 2080, the number of "normal" working hours per year, and we get a whopping hourly wage of $1.73. Man! What a deal!

So this is what reparations are all about. Black farmers, who work much more than the normal eight-hour day, who have been discriminated against by the government for 14 years and probably longer, who have been literally driven out of business because of rising costs and insurmountable debt are now paid $1.73 per hour. If this is reparation for Black people, we are in deep trouble.

President Clinton said the settlement was an important step in "ongoing efforts to rid the Agriculture Department of discriminatory behavior and redress any harm that has been caused by past discrimination against African-American family farmers." I'd say it's a very small step, a baby step in fact, when it comes to repairing the damage done since 1983.

Some Black farmers, even after having their government debt forgiven, still owe money to private banks and finance companies. One farmer said he owed an additional

$42,000.00. Well, after his reparation payment from Uncle Sam he should have just enough money left to get him in debt once again.

Black farmers have suffered tremendously over the years while many white farmers and mega-farming corporations have benefited greatly from government subsidy programs and the like. With this settlement Black farmers will continue to suffer—or, as many have done and are still doing, go out of the farming business all together, unless we decide to help.

Black people spend millions of dollars each year on food. Black farmers have been going down the economic drain for years. What's wrong with this picture?

According to **Urban Call**, a retail magazine published by Segmented Marketing Services, Inc. in Winston-Salem, North Carolina, there are only nineteen Black-owned supermarkets in the entire country. According to the **Harvest Institute**, a Washington DC-based think tank founded by Dr. Claud Anderson, Black farmers once owned millions of acres of land. Now they own about 400,000 acres.

Echoes of Booker T. Washington's admonishment to his people to be producers rather than consumers ring so true. We are buying most of our food from someone other than Black farmers who are steadily being driven out of business by the government.

Many of us will walk by a Black-owned grocery store to get to one owned by a non-Black. Those of us who own stores will not seek ways to support Black farmers by seeing that, to the degree possible, our products are purchased from Black-owned farms. We should take a lesson from the **REACH** Program in Meridian, Mississippi.

I am not saying that nothing is being done; I am saying that not enough is being done. We eat too much food in this country for our farmers to be going out of business. I understand there are economies to consider and new technology in farming that must be instituted in order to compete. But who do we think was first to devise "new economies" and "new technologies" in farming at the turn of the century? Can you say Dr. George Washington Carver?

Reparations for Black farmers? I don't think so. What they got was a slap in the face. What can they do? No, what can we do? Take the time to write to your Congressperson. Look at ways in which your community can support Black farmers by buying their products. Create vertical businesses in the food industry that, in turn, create jobs not only in farming but also in trucking, storage, processing, distribution, warehousing, and retail.

What can we do? Support one another much more than we do now. Our economic destiny depends upon it.

Black Farmers Still Fighting

Get land and lie on it. Those were the words of Booker T. Washington as he counseled his people toward ownership of the most valuable commodity in the world. Brother Washington went on to tell his people, "You go to town with your pockets full and your wagons empty and return with your wagons full and your pockets empty. You must go to town with your wagons full of your produce and your pockets empty, and return with your pockets full and your wagons empty."

This was one of the most basic principles anyone could promulgate. It made sense then and it makes sense now. As we see Black farmers still struggling to retain a modicum of what once was theirs, and as we witness them in their fight to maintain some level of economic dignity, Booker T's words ring clear. Black farmers heeded those words, despite having their land stolen from them, being denied loans from the government, and being patted on their heads with a ridiculous monetary offer to kiss and make up with the United States Department of Agriculture. Black farmers took the risks and stayed the course. Now, what are we going to do to assist them in their fight for economic justice?

According to leading expert, Dr. Robert D. Bullard, in 1910 Black farmers owned over 16 million acres of farmland. Ten years later some 925,000 Black farmers tilled the soil and fed our people—and other people as well. Now we have fewer than 17,000 Black farmers who own less than 3 million acres of land.

In case you did not hear about the proposed settlement offered to Black farmers back in March 1999, it was an insult to them. The farmers are still fighting for an equitable end to a long and hard-fought battle with the USDA that saw years of blatant discrimination against Black farmers and their families.

The sad footnote to this case is the specter of billions per year being spent on food by Black people in this country every year. Add that to the mere nineteen Black-owned supermarkets in this country and you will see a picture of irresponsibility, complacency, and downright dependency by Black people on the very basics needed to sustain life.

This scenario also presents an opportunity, as most problems do. As we always say in our newspaper column, if we would pool our resources and establish more super-markets—and support them, of course—we could take a huge chunk out of our problem. Additionally, if we would develop vertical businesses in the food industry, similar to what Dr. Claud Anderson has been telling us for years, we could create more jobs for our people and we could support our farmers by buying their products. Now that's as simple as it gets, folks. We're talking about food, something each of us must have.

Of course, this will also work with other items like fish and chicken. Anything we eat, we should be able to provide it for ourselves. It's pretty scary to think that some-one else controls our food supply. It's also pretty sad that we could not, if pressed to do so, feed our own children.

Well, that's why the Black farmers are so vital to Black people in general. They are the ones who own most of the land, and since no one is making more of that valuable commodity we must see that they are able to hold on to what they have—and get more if they can.

Some may say farming is passé and no one wants to do it any more. Well, until eating becomes passé and goes out of style we had better have a few Black farmers to rely upon to grow our food.

We should take a lesson from the REACH Program in Meridian, Mississippi, which, since 1977, has been practic-ing what many of us only preach about. Members of the Christ Temple Church, under the leadership of Bishop Luke Edwards, pooled their food stamps, bought peanuts and sold them on the streets. In 1999, REACH owns 4,000 acres of land, a hog farm, 1000 head of cattle, an auto repair business, a construction company, three motels, four restaurants, a K-12 school with dormitories, and (wouldn't you know it?) a supermarket. REACH is taking care of business, and one of the main ingredients in its success is land ownership.

In an exclusive interview of a Black farmer conducted by Dr. Bullard for the Environmental Justice Resource Center, Mr. Gary Grant of Tillery, North Carolina had this to say when asked how we can help. "I would like Black institutions and Black people to believe that Black farmers know what is needed. Second, I would also like them to contribute financially, morally, physically, and spiritually. Third, we need to begin a massive education program with our children of the importance of owning land."

Mr. Grant also seemed to echo old Booker T. when he said, "Land ownership is economic power, political power, and is the only avenue that we really have to ensure our children a legacy." Now, if you don't believe Gary Grant, dig out those old records and listen to James Brown when he says, *Let's get together and get some land; raise our food like the man.*

Flipping the Script

We hear and read a great deal about Black people and our buying practices. We see calls for boycotts against certain companies and stores, some are calling for selective buying campaigns, and others are asking us to refrain from spending our money for a day or two or for a certain holiday season.

Some of these initiatives are called to make a point to those who take our money and disrespect us at the same time. Some campaigns are pushed to show White América and other ethnic groups the real economic impact of Black consumers. That's all well and good, but imagine what would happen if the script were flipped. What would Black people do if the companies and stores we are trying to hurt decided to stop selling their products and services to us?

A sobering thought, isn't it? Yes, suppose all of the non-Black owned companies like supermarkets, clothing stores, shoe stores, drug stores, movie theaters, lottery outlets, liquor stores, restaurants, hotels and motels, department stores, and all of the other thousands of businesses patronized by Black people simply said, "We are no longer selling to Black people."

Legal arguments aside, if that happened tomorrow could Black people feed our own children? Would we be able to provide them with clothing? Would we be able to obtain the medicines necessary for our elderly and infirm? Would we be able to clean our homes? Would we be able to hold our annual *soirées* at those fine hotels we love so much? Would we be able to hold our family reunions at those small motels in the south that are almost exclusively owned by people from India and Pakistan?

What would we do? Some of us would immediately resort to that old strategy of forcing businesses owned by others to "take" our money. We would petition the government to "make" those nasty companies open their doors to our dollars and accept them. We would demand they take our money and give us the "privilege" of doing business with them—despite the glaring fact that they want nothing to do with us.

Others of us would take another path. We would put our money together and start our own businesscs. We would contact our Black farmer brothers and sisters and set up purchasing agreements and food co-ops. We would call Curtis Dean, Bill Wilson, John Brown, Mabra Holeyfield, and Charles McAfee to help us build our own hotels and motels. We would talk to Earvin "Magic" Johnson about bringing his theaters to our neighborhoods. We would call for an economic summit with our business leaders and seek their counsel on building profitable corporations.

Those of us who are conscious when it comes to supporting our own, and loving our own, and trusting our own, would contact Ken Bridges and Al Wellington to discover a new way of re-directing our consumption spending toward one another via the MATAH Network. Our brothers and sisters who understand what true economic empowerment is would immediately call Dr. Claud Anderson and bring him to our cities to set up vertically integrated Black owned businesses.

Some of our brothers and sisters, sadly, would see the refusal by these companies to sell to Black people as a serious problem—and, admittedly, initially it would be. But if that was the case and we could do nothing about it legally, would it be wise to whine about it and beg those businesses to please take our $500 billion?

Other brothers and sisters would see this development as an exceptional opportunity. We would move swiftly to the self-sufficiency we must have to survive in this country. We would develop the "communities" we so often talk about, by building the infrastructure necessary for our economic foundation. We would jump at the "opportunity" to finally stop spending 95% of our annual income with others. And we would grasp the challenge, pick up the gauntlct, and move forward, doing what we must do to truly empower ourselves.

They say out of crisis comes opportunity. By flipping the script, whether imagined or real, we are able to see the possibilities for Black people. We are also able to peer into the depths of our economic situation in this country. By flipping the script Black brothers and sisters can, if we so desire, finally do what we have been instructed to do by our forefathers and mothers—do for self and spend as much of our money as possible among our own people.

Flipping the mental script on our Black *anti-buying* tactics and looking at them as White (and others) *anti-selling* responses will open our minds to our innate talents and intellect, and it will force us to respond in-kind. It will slap us in our collective face and say, "Black people, it's time you start to take your $500 billion and do something for yourselves and for your children." It will ask us, "Are 19 Black owned supermarkets in this entire country enough to feed our people?" It will make us realize that until we build our own hotels and other facilities we will always be at the economic mercy of those who own them.

Man, what an opportunity. Flip your script and let's get busy doing what we must do to get our true freedom. And we had better get busy before the script is really flipped.

Political Divisiveness or Economic Solidarity?

What are you? A Republican? A Democrat? A Liberal? A Conservative? The "silly season" came and the big parties were held in Philadelphia and Los Angeles. Black people were hyped about the upcoming election to the point that it was all we heard about for days. Black people were so happy to be "in the house" with the political movers and shakers that we were diverted yet again from our economic mission.

Black talk shows are rife with who's on what side of the political fence, which Blacks are in which party, and which Black people are in whose camp. We see Black people standing on the stages lauding their candidates, promoting the virtues of their party, and promulgating "inclusiveness" for Black people. We see Black people skinnin' and grinnin,' entertaining the conventioneers, and enjoying the hoopla associated with what will inevitably be a return to business as usual in January 2001.

Black people are convening forums to "discuss" political strategies, political fairness, political candidates, and the political future of Black children, all without having one ounce of real political power. All of the Black politicians in Washington combined cannot pass one law. Therefore, they must trust the white leaders of the party to "do the right thing" for them and their people. More times than not, they are and we are double-crossed. When that happens we return to our "Drive the Vote," "Rock the Vote," and Rap the Vote" campaigns, because "this time" we will hold them accountable.

How can we hold politicians accountable? The answer given most of the time is: "By voting them out of office." That could be true in a few extreme cases, but some of the worst politicians for Black people have been in office for years and years—case-in-point, Jesse Helms and Strom Thurmond. So much for accountability, and even if we did vote them out, we will have suffered under their rule for two, four, or six years. We do not have that kind of time, folks.

The political hucksters put on one face from August to November and another face after January. Four years later it happens all over again. Why are we so available to the political parties and their lackeys to do their bidding and to promote their agendas? Why do we work ourselves into a frenzy about political games, for which Black people make none of the rules, only to be mistreated, ignored, and taken for granted by them—both parties—after they get what they want from us?

The watchword for every political campaign in the Black community is "Vote." Of course, preceding that word, the call goes out for Black people to "Register." That's all well and good, but there is much more for us to do after we vote. We must work, for ourselves and among ourselves, and not go home to wait for white folks to take care of us and do what they promised to do.

One of the largest political forums ever took place during the 2000 Democratic Convention in Los Angeles. Listening to the list of Black "who's who" made me wonder how we can convene such a group of wealthy, well known, respected, and influential brothers and sisters to discuss politics, and not get these same folks together to discuss and take action on economic empowerment for Black people.

This distinctive panel of Black people comprised the intellect and the resources necessary to start an economic movement for the ages. Instead, much of their time was spent discussing politics. Don't get me wrong. We must participate in politics, but we must never do it to the neglect of economics. The establishment wants us to spend our time on something that will keep us from making any change in our economic status, because that would mean we would begin to re-direct our money away from them and toward ourselves.

We cannot allow our brothers and sisters to forget the words of Marcus Garvey, who said, *The most important area for the exercise of independent effort [is] economic. After a people have established a firm industrial foundation they naturally turn to politics... but not first to... politics, because the latter cannot exist without the former.*

We must heed the words of T. Thomas Fortune, who told us, *No people ever became great and prosperous by devoting their infant energies to politics. We were literally born into political responsibility before we had mastered the economic conditions which underlie these duties.*

When asked what Black people needed most, Booker T. Washington said, *Economic solidarity!* Shirley Chisholm said, *Our bondage and our battle is economic. We have to spend more time at economic conferences, be producers and provide jobs. The answer is economic self-sufficiency.*

I submit to you, my dear brothers and sisters, that the answer is still economics—not politics. I pray that the distinguished panel I mentioned will also see that our problem is economic and spend much of its time dealing with strategies that will move our people away from the broken promises and empty victories of politics. I hope the panel will agree to get back together and stay together and devote more of its resources—financial and intellectual—to serve and lead us to and through a new paradigm for economic solidarity.

Hobnobbing with the politicians, being elected to office, and participating in conventions are fine. But those kinds of activities should not dominate our thinking and our actions so much that we forget about the importance of economic empowerment.

We must not allow ourselves to be divided by political parties; we must work together, politically, no matter what party we prefer. Moreover, Black people must work hard, even harder than we do for the politicians, to secure our own economic solidarity. Politics alone will not take us where we need to go. Politics, placed before economics, will result in the same problems we have faced for the past forty years. Politics divides us; economics will make us whole.

Our Collective Victory

We are free to begin the awesome task of nation building. But the task of building healthier, more prosperous Black communities all over America begins with each individual. It is the private dreams and efforts of individuals multiplied geometrically that will give the whole race an uplift.
Michael Grant

O death, where is thy sting? O grave, where is thy victory?
1 Corinthians 15:55

We cannot be afraid of the challenge to win, and we must be willing to pay the price of victory. With each problem comes an opportunity, and with opportunity comes challenge. We must accept the challenge of solving our problems and make the most of the inherent opportunity within that problem. Let's look at solutions.

There are three economic solution-oriented entities with which I am involved, although there are several around the country that I promote in my writings and speeches. The three are: Powernomics, the Richard Allen Foundation, and the MATAH Network. The others include the R.E.A.C.H. Project in Meridian, Mississippi, Recycling Black Dollars in Los Angeles, California, the economic self-sufficiency efforts of the Nation of Islam, and of course all of the positive Black owned businesses and organizations that advocate and practice economic empowerment.

I could not have written all of these words without offering some solution to the economic quagmire in which we find ourselves. I hope you will take heed of the examples that follow and act upon their principles. Get involved. Don't just hang your head in disgust or be lulled into complacency. Do something!

My final caveat is this. There is a big difference between feeling good and doing good. In my opinion, we place too much emphasis on the emotional and far too little on the pragmatic. By doing good we can also do well—for all of us.

If you have read everything in this book thus far, you have an excellent idea of what we as Black people must do to get our true freedom, both psychological and economic. Here are some opportunities for you to be part of the solution rather than part of the problem. I pray you will use them.

Attaining True Freedom – The MATAH Network

Ownership and control are most important when it comes to economic empowerment. Various products that are manufactured by Black people, if not controlled by Black people, will soon fall prey to Black consumer exploitation. We have seen it many times over with Black people. When will it end?

For example, many brands of Black hair care products were being developed and manufactured during the 1980's. Also during those years, some Black-owned companies were sold, and several new products that mimicked Black-owned hair care products were introduced. The American Health and Beauty Aids Institute (AHBAI) was established and started a collective effort to head-off the corporate attacks on Black hair care manufacturers as well as the marketing and advertising charades being perpetrated upon the Black consumer.

Approximately 15 years later we have an industry that is 100% Black, on the consumer side, but minimally owned and controlled by Black people. Virtually every dollar that is spent on the retail end of the Black hair care product chain comes from Black consumers—billions of dollars every year! Yet on the manufacturing side and especially on the distribution side Black businesses are reaping comparatively little of that bountiful harvest.

Why do we not have control of the distribution of our own products, especially those we manufacture? How could we have lost control, if we ever had it at all, of one of the most lucrative industries in the Black community? Could it be that we were not educated about the brands that were Black-owned? (AHBAI came up with the Proud Lady logo to solve that problem.) Could it have been because we were lured away from Black businesses and Black products because they cost a few cents more? Or, could it be that we just did not have the proper level of Black consciousness necessary to cause us to support our own people?

The situation in which we find ourselves now, buying the bulk of our own hair care products from someone other than a Black person, suggests we have lost a significant battle in this arena. We have seen the demise of other Black owned businesses and products, and in recent years there has been a foray into the Black funeral industry as well. Hair care, funeral homes, and restaurants should be the last businesses we are willing to give to someone else, but with the way things are going... well, I just pray it will not happen.

What can we do? Have you ever heard of the **MATAH Network**? It's an organization comprising individuals who are *consciously committed* to a *race first* philosophy and dedicated to re-directing our spending toward one another. **MATAH** is an organization that stresses a level of Black consciousness that will cause us to do what every other group in this country strives to do: own, control, and support a portion of our own economy and not allow others to come in and snatch it away.

Those of us who are **"MATAH"** understand the sacrifice and dedication necessary for our people to have true freedom. The **MATAH** practice love, trust, and mutual support for our race. The **MATAH** is too busy buying and selling Black manufactured and distributed products to have time to be jealous or envious of our brothers and sisters. The men and women of **MATAH** are principled, learned, and staunchly unapologetic when it comes to knowing who we are, from whence we came, and where we must go. The **MATAH** is the personification of strength, determination, and willingness to do what it takes to gain true freedom.

The **MATAH** will not sell out to the highest bidder because we know how important ownership and control of resources are to the very survival of our people. **MATAH** addresses the psychological barriers and shortcomings of our people when it comes to productivity, distribution, and consumption. **MATAH** feeds the mind and the spirit with writings from some of our greatest Black educators and thinkers. **MATAH** prepares our bodies and keeps them healthy because we cannot fight if we are weak and infirm. **MATAH** is holistic in its approach to economic empowerment; it covers all of the bases—spiritual, mental, physical, educational.

Simply, **MATAH** is *Those people of African descent who know that practicing a race-first philosophy is the key to true freedom for African people and who refuse to have that spirit crushed.* Are you **MATAH**? If so, please contact me and be an active and conscious member of our race who is dedicated to the basic economic principles of ownership and control of our resources and re-directing our tremendous consumption-spending toward one another. Get involved in an effort that will help propel us to the heights that Black people deserve and must achieve very soon.

By the way, just think what would happen if Black owned hair care products was distributed through the **MATAH** Network. We complain about someone else controlling the channels of distribution for our hair care products. Are we willing to use our own distribution system instead? It's there waiting for you, Black barbers, manufacturers, wholesalers, retailers, cosmetologists, and consumers.

If you are **MATAH**, then I know you will do what is right. I ask you again. **Are you MATAH?**

Wake Up, My People, Please!

In my book, **Economic Empowerment or Economic Enslavement – We have a choice**, I discuss the notion of our people being asleep and each time the alarm goes off we roll over and push that snooze button. Well we've all heard the saying, "If you snooze, you lose." That saying could not be truer than it is today when it comes to Black people - my people.

Dr. Claud Anderson, author of **Black Labor – White Wealth**, has been traveling the length and breadth of this country for the past seven years telling us that we had better wake up and smell the coffee. He warned us at every turn that we had only a few years left to establish ourselves economically. He has literally shed tears during some of his presentations at the stone-cold facts regarding Black poverty, inequity, and the collective economic position of Black people in this country.

Dr. Anderson begged us to awaken from our deep sleep and get busy building vertically integrated businesses that would create jobs for our people, help feed our people, help our people to become more self-sufficient, and build wealth in our neighborhoods. He told us that if we did those things we would then—and only then—have real communities.

I remember hearing him at a lecture in Cincinnati in 1997 when he warned that Black people had only two and a half more years, at best, to get it together. He said that by then we would be faced with the stark reality of social, demographic, and economic changes unlike any we had ever seen in this country. It was sad that we have been in this country since the early 1600's and worked to build these United States to what they are today, Dr. Anderson told us. But, there we were in 1997, having virtually marched in place for the last forty years.

Are we still marching in place? Please, there's no need for you to answer that. Many of us are still slumbering, rolling over and hitting that snooze button on the alarm clock, saying let me sleep for just a while longer. Well, now we have slept too long. Dr. Anderson's prediction has become a reality. Black people are being surpassed, not only by people whose first language is Spanish, but also by Asians and Native Americans as well.

Nothing against our other ethnic brothers and sisters; they are simply taking care of their business and, as the kids say, "I ain't mad at 'em." That's all we have been trying to get our people to do. That's all Dr. Claud Anderson has been talking about. He told us that we would soon find ourselves on the outside looking in at someone else's economy. In case you have not been keeping up with the latest news, you are in for a rude awakening (pun intended).

One network dedicated at least one half its 30-minute prime time news program to the rising tide of Latinos in this country. When asked if Latinos were moving toward the "mainstream," Peter Jennings said they are already in the "mainstream." In addition, Geraldo Rivera recently did a show on the influence and affluence of Hispanics in this country, citing their rise to the top in many areas of endeavor. And finally, there was a meeting—an economic summit—in New York recently during which several Hispanic leaders came together to discuss economic empowerment.

Also, during the Jennings' feature, individual Latinos referred to themselves as having been discriminated against and treated unfairly, especially since 1960, in this country. They suggested, with conviction, that they deserve to be recognized for their achievements, that they were sick and tired of being treated unfairly, and they are determined to take their rightful place in this country. (Sound familiar?) Forty years of discrimination, and Latinos are making their case, and backing it up, by working together toward a common economic goal rather than making a beeline to the nearest political office.

Black people have been in this country ten times as long. What do we deserve for the discrimination we have suffered? Where are our reparations for our free labor? When will Peter Jennings say Black people are already in the "mainstream"? And what are we willing to do to gain our rightful place in this country? Have we sought political gain rather than economic strength to our own detriment? We are sleeping while others are passing us by—albeit, in some cases, with the aid, assistance, and encouragement of the majority.

That's exactly what Dr. Anderson has been saying would happen. Please keep in mind that he never said anything against others doing what they are supposed to do economically. Rather, he always told us what WE should do. Too bad we did not listen— and act upon his message.

This country is rapidly changing. People of Latin descent, probably to the delight of the majority and as a *lesser of two evils* alternative to Black people, are moving in and moving up. They are mobilizing and pooling their resources to carve out and build their own economy. They are making bold statements in business, entertainment, and politics. And as Dr. Anderson literally cried at the terrible economic conditions of Black people in New Orleans, he cited the facts about what lay ahead relative to our overall economic position in this country. Well, that time has come. Question: How will we respond?

As we are faced with fighting not only the power brokers in the majority community but also those Black people who, (In the words of Dr. Anderson) can be classified as Hayward Sheppards and Sambos, we have a rough ride ahead. But we can achieve what we must by implementing the very simple strategy of mutual support and collective/cooperative economics. We see it all around us with other groups, our unique history in this country notwithstanding.

We must carve out niches in those industries in which our consumption is dominant. We must learn to own and control the entire business chain—from the natural resource to retail. We must be smarter with our dollars and rather than continue to give them away without reciprocity, we must pool them and make them work for our people. And most of all, if we are going to achieve our goal of true freedom and economic empowerment, we must throw off the psychological chains that bind us. We must distance ourselves from those who would sound the alarm as Sheppard did at Harper's Ferry, and simply make "us" more important than "I."

Contact the **Harvest Institute**, (Washington, DC) headed by Dr. Claud Anderson, read his books, **Black Labor, White Wealth, Powernomics,** and **Dirty Little Secrets,** and subscribe, promote, and support Dr. Anderson's *Powernomics* business development strategies for Black people.

As I said at the beginning of this article, "Wake up and smell the coffee." It definitely has a *Juan Valdez* bouquet, and unless we are ready to make our own coffee, we had better acquire a taste for theirs real soon.

It's Time For Ownership!

That's the overriding theme promoted by the Richard Allen Foundation (RAF), an organization that is, in fact, practicing the "To Seek for Ourselves" slogan adopted by Peter Williams, Absalom Jones, and Richard Allen and created by The Free African Society in the 1700's.

The main thrust of the RAF is to build the Black economy by building and owning hotels across this country. Via RAF's *Visions 2000 Plan*, Black people will have the opportunity to actually have individual investments in these hotels, thus own a piece of the pie in this burgeoning industry in which Black people have all but disappeared as owners.

Hotel ownership will have a tremendous economic impact on the lives of Black people. Just think of the ancillary benefits that will accrue in the areas of employment, vending, equipment and supplies, maintenance, and all of the services necessary to operate and manage a hotel. The possibilities are virtually limitless.

Mr. John Brown, Treasurer of RAF, says, "African Americans spend billions of dollars in the hotel industry each year. Why should we continue to dump our money into this bottomless pit and be at the mercy of whimsical room-rate fluctuations and rising bed taxes and not get into the game ourselves?"

Curtis Dean, one of the highest ranking executives in the Marriott Corporation, also sings from that hymn book. He states, "Black people are missing out on an industry that is virtually recession-proof. Because we do not own the primary brick and mortar assets of the travel and tourism industry, we are continually losing out on an excellent vehicle to build wealth in our communities."

The Richard Allen Foundation is doing what many of us just give lip-service to: Collective and cooperative economics. The folks at RAF have started a movement, an economic movement that will propel us forward and recapture a niche we once had with the Manse Hotel in Cincinnati,

Ohio, the Moulon Rouge, in Las Vegas, the Wells' Built Hotel in Orlando, Florida and the hundreds of other Black owned hotel properties that existed from the turn of the 20th century until the 1960's.

Yes, we can restore what we once had, if we get on board with organizations like the RAF and work in con-owned hotels and other economic empowering entities are the keys to the economic freedom we "seek for ourselves." All we need to do, considering our collective wealth, is get involved on whatever individual level we choose, take control of our resources, and build some new pyramids.

Ernestine Lee Henning, Founder and Chair of RAF, says, "If we are to move our economic position to a higher level... we must focus on ownership. Demonstrations for 'rights' alone just gain us more opportunities to consume more while others reap the real gains. There can be no parity without ownership."

C'mon, folks. We know the deal. We know that more than 60% of the small motel industry is owned by people from India and Pakistan; we also know those people are doing quite well. After all, we stay in their motels and hotels, especially in small southern towns, during our family reunions and on other occasions.

We know that Black people, despite the few forward-thinking brothers and sisters who own hotels and motels, are hardly a blip on the radar screen of hotel ownership. We know that each year millions of Black people travel to various cities for conferences, church conventions, and entertainment events.

We know the leisure industry is hardly ever affected by recessions and downturns in the economy. We know that Black people spend proportionately more of our disposable income in this industry than others. Finally, we know that we have a half-trillion dollars each year.

Knowing all of these things, we must use our intellect, our financial resources, and our ingenuity to help *Visions 2000* in its quest to build hotels in which our children and grandchildren—and anyone else—can stay. Call

The Richard Allen Foundation in Inglewood, California, and be a Founding Sponsor of the *Visions 2000* Program. Get in on the ground floor of this innovative approach to economic empowerment.

Catch the vision! Richard Allen would be proud.

Cleaning Up!

I am about to share a simple strategy that, if followed, will help propel Black people to higher economic heights. It's a simple strategy—a very simple strategy—one that will probably make you ask, "Why haven't we done something like this before?" While there are very good reasons for that, we are at a point now where we as Black people in this country can affect tremendous change in our economic destiny. This strategy is only the beginning of that very necessary change.

There are two things we absolutely must do to reverse our current collective economic situation: Reach a higher level of Black consciousness and re-direct just a portion of our consumption spending toward Black-owned businesses.

The first ideal is psychologically based. A greater knowledge and appreciation of whom we are and what we must do to get our true freedom will inevitably cause a drastic change in our collective behavior. And consumerism depends, to a great degree, upon behavior.

Simply put, Black people must change our behavior when it comes to what, when, how, and why we purchase products and services. We must elevate the act of purchasing to a conscious—not an unconscious—decision. We must understand that no matter how much money we have or how little we have, when we spend that money we are creating wealth for someone else. Our spending habits, or spending behavior, must be supported by education and a consciousness that causes us to critically consider the ramifications of spending 95% of our hard-earned dollars with businesses other than our own.

Many companies and individuals are and have been "cleaning up" on our dollars for many years. Don't you think it's time we put a stop to the madness of a people who earn $500 billion per year always finding itself at the bottom of the economic ladder? Isn't it time we stop simply complaining about various companies discriminating against us and not serving us and calling us names and not promoting us and not putting us on their boards?

Isn't it time we turn the tables and start doing some "cleaning up" of our own? Here's how we start. If you get the latest copy of **Black Buying Power,** published by **Target Market News** report you will see numerous categories of products and services that Black people spend tremendous amounts of money on each year. If you single out one category, household cleaning products, you will notice that Black people spend more than $1 billion on various items from soap powder to pine cleaner to laundry detergent and all of the other things we use daily around our homes.

Now here is the real kicker. If you have not heard, we do have a Black-owned, Black-operated, and Black-controlled corporation called the **MATAH** Network, Inc. that manufacturers, warehouses, distributes, and sells house-hold cleaners—the same kinds of cleaners you and I buy from those companies we complain about so often. Are you getting the picture yet? Is it becoming clearer?

Well, picture this. If Black people simply, and I emphasize **"simply,"** change our purchasing habits from those household cleaners we have bought for generations and buy the **MATAH** cleaning products, we will have created the largest single Black owned business in the world! I am talking about a $1.4 billion business in one category of one industry. How's that for cleaning up?

One simple act, one simple purchase can be the beginning of real economic freedom for our people. This is not difficult; it is not brain surgery. It is not something we need to research, ponder, strategize, or have meetings about. This is probably the simplest thing we can do for ourselves to get our freedom, and if we are not willing to do this, how can we continue to discuss anything else when it comes to economic empowerment?

A mere change in our behavior, the same thing many of our brothers and sisters have been telling us for years, is our key to economic freedom. It can start with simple soap products and move to other goods and services from there.

There is no need for comparative analysis, folks; basically bubbles are bubbles. But for those doubting Thomases, and I know you are out there, **MATAH** products are not only better than the others you currently buy, they are also a better buy. You get more for your money.

So do your comparison if you must. As for me, my level of Black consciousness is such that I do not need to do that. I have made it a habit to seek out and support Black-owned businesses. I have made a commitment to stop complaining about other folks' stuff and get my own stuff. For those reasons and others, I am **MATAH**, which means *People of African descent who know that practicing a race first philosophy is the key to obtaining true freedom for African people – and who refuse to have that spirit crushed.* Are you **MATAH**?

The **MATAH** Network, established by Al Wellington and Ken Bridges, with the assistance of Dr. Edward Robinson, author of ***Journey of the Songhai People***, has made its initial mark on several thousand brothers and sisters across this country. It is now moving to its next level of evolution. Cleaning products are just one of the hundreds of items offered by the **MATAH** Network. Check out the website, **MATAH**.com, and see for yourself.

Whether you are **MATAH** or not, please look in the mirror and see if you are Black. If you are, please buy **MATAH** cleaning products and let's start right here right now, with a simple act of purchasing that will bring us the greatest economic leverage Black people have ever seen in this country. Let's start "cleaning up" for a change—with our own cleaning products. And then let's move on from there.

Kudos to Black Americans - *A Reprise*

When I wrote **"Kudos to Black Americans"** little did I know it would soon circulate throughout the world on the Internet. It was just another column on Economic Empowerment and among the hundreds I have written for the National Newspaper Publishers Association.

During the past two years I have received **"The Letter"** via Internet from friends across the country with notes such as, "Have you seen this?" "Check this out!" "This is deep—a must read!" Most people did not know who wrote the piece because when a Philadelphia newspaper put it on the Internet, no author was noted.

Now **"The Letter"** is now in books; it is on a videotaped sermon by Dr. Fred Price; it has been packaged and is being circulated around the country by Drs. Julia and Nathan Hare. **"The Letter,"** referred to in some circles as the antidote for the Willie (Lynch) Chip, has certainly caused a stir among our people. Controversial? Yes. Thought-provoking? Most assuredly. Eye-opening? Definitely. True? You can be the judge of that.

The main reason for writing **"The Letter"** was to make my people understand and deal with our economic situation. It reaches back into history and carries the reader through a series of events, and it simply says "Thank You" for all of the things Black people have done for all other Americans. **"The Letter"** takes us to a place most of us do not want to go, but it encourages us, as we leave that place, to move to a higher, more responsible, more enlightened place, and to be more determined to do for self.

By the end of **"The Letter"** we are left drained, confused, angry, inspired, and every other feeling along the emotional continuum. Some people, after having read it, decided to change some things in their lives. Some people made excuses for their inappropriate behavior and sent messages to me rationalizing why they had to continue down the same economic path we have traveled for 35 years.

Whatever your reaction, whatever your emotion, I hope you really understood the gravity of our situation in this country. I hope you asked, "What can I do now?" That's what this revisit to **"The Letter"** is all about: It is an answer to that question and presents a vehicle through which we can change our collective economic condition.

There are two things we must do in order to change our current economic status. First, we must change our minds. In other words, we must get our psychological freedom. Then we must re-direct our consumption spending toward one another, instead of continuing to give our dollars to others.

Now, the million dollar questions: How do we do that? By what means? I have listed several vehicles through which Black people can achieve the economic goals we seek. All we need to do is follow them, join them, and support them.

The next question: What are you going to do to help change our collective economic position? We understand that every slave did not want to go with Harriet Tubman. We understand that we are not all at the same place at the same time, and that's all right, because all it takes is a small percentage of our people to accomplish something great. Everyone else will either get involved later or benefit from that greatness as it evolves. So, what are you doing?

Please reread *"Kudos to Black Americans."* Understand what it is saying to you, to our people. Understand that if we do not change, we will remain in the clutches of *Willie Lynch*. Also understand that even though we have come through so much and suffered so much in this country, we can overcome our condition simply by raising our consciousness and re-directing a greater portion of our consumption spending toward our own people. That's pretty simple, isn't it?

Those of us who have asked for a solution to our problems and a vehicle through which we can reach our goal of economic empowerment, those of us who are tired of the empty rhetoric, the "rap and clap" sessions, the "talk and walk" political strategies, let's get to work. We have much work to do and many resources with which to do that work. I look forward to it. How about you?

Epilogue

All hard work brings a profit, but mere talk leads only to poverty.
Proverbs 14:23

What Are You Waiting For?

Remember that famous saying? "If not now, when? If not you, who?" That's what we face when it comes to economic empowerment and true freedom for Black people. Too often we pray for solutions to our dilemmas only to look around and see that we already have the answers right in our midst.

We must learn to use the resources we have—our tremendous resources, to take care of ourselves and our children. And if we do not make that move now, after more than 100 years of pleading and admonishing by our ancestors, when are we going to get it done? If we do not take it upon ourselves, individually, to make the requisite sacrifices and do the things that will move us forward, who will do it?

My Brothers and Sisters, please take these words and turn them into action. The way to psychological and economic freedom, the subtitle of this book, has been laid before you. If you and I fail to adhere to these basic principles, we will forever be held accountable for our apathy and lack of progress as well as our failure to leave an economic legacy for our progeny. That would be shameful.

I ask again: ***If not now, when? If not you, who?***

BOOK AVAILABLE THROUGH
Milligan Books
An Imprint Of Professional Business
Consulting Service
BLACKONOMICS$ $14.95

Order Form

Milligan Books
1425 West Manchester, Suite B,
Los Angeles, California 90047
(323) 750-3592

Mail Check or Money Order to:
Milligan Books

Name _____ Date _____

Address _____

City_____ State _____ Zip Code_____

Day telephone _____

Evening telephone_____

Book title _____

Number of books ordered ___ Total cost .... $ _____

Sales Taxes (CA Add 8%) .... $ _____

Shipping & Handling $3.55 per book .... $ _____

Total Amount Due..$ _____

☐Check   ☐Money Order   Other Cards _____

☐ Visa   ☐ Master Card   Expiration Date _____

Credit Card No. _____

Driver's License No. _____

_____   _____

Signature   Date